THE NEW YORK BOTANICAL GARDEN

THE NEW YORK BOTANICAL GARDEN

EDITED BY
Gregory Long
AND
Anne Skillion

WITH ESSAYS BY
Kim E. Tripp
Todd Forrest
Gregory Long
Barbara M. Thiers
Susan Fraser

ART DIRECTION BY
Marilan Lund

ABRAMS / NEW YORK

CONTENTS

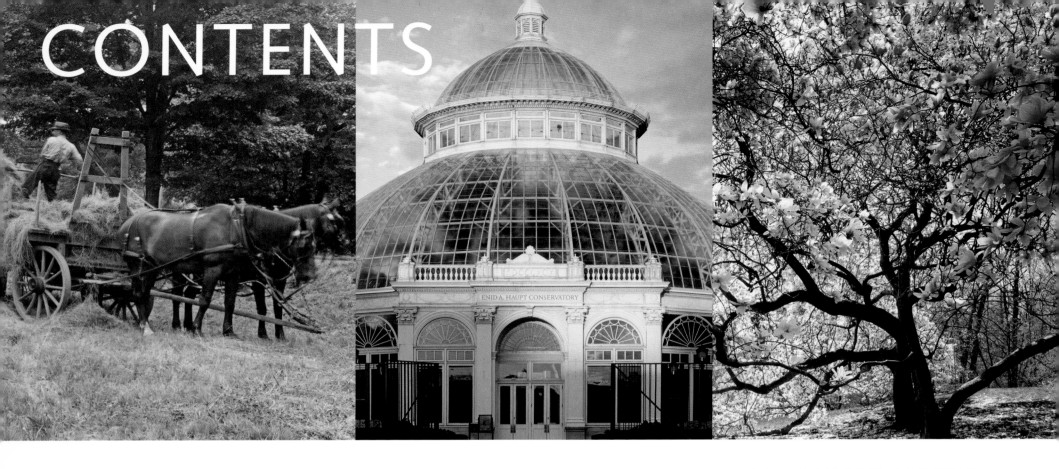

Since the beginning of civilization, people have strived to understand the diversity of living forms around them. Plants in particular, because of their vital importance and captivating beauty, are central to human life. The modern botanical garden, of which the New York Botanical Garden is a premier example, is the most advanced form of institution devoted to them. —Edward O. Wilson

For more than a century, the professional horticulturists, plant scientists, and educators of the New York Botanical Garden have worked successfully to build a comprehensive organization with three interlocking reasons for being. First, New York City needs a place of beauty and quiet, an oasis of calm and civility, not a park but a designed landscape where people can enjoy the greatest triumphs of nature. Designated a National Historic Landmark, with collections comprising more than one million living plants—including thirty thousand mature trees that have been protected and carefully tended since the late nineteenth century, thousands of tropical and desert plants that visitors can see nowhere else in New York, and many unrivaled features, such as the most beautiful rose garden in America—the Botanical Garden exhibits nature at its best.

Second, the world's nations, universities, and conservation organizations need as much information as can be uncovered about the plants of the world. The New York Botanical Garden has always been a research institution with an outstanding faculty and graduate students striving to expand humankind's knowledge of plants and to disseminate that new knowledge. Generations of botanical scientists have amassed here a distinguished, unbroken record of scholarly research and teaching about plants and their uses by people.

Third, the children of New York and their teachers need our help and guidance in order to better understand plants and their habitats, their adaptations, value, historical significance, and status as endangered species. The Garden is an educational institution serving many constituencies.

This unique place is celebrated for the drama of its topography, the scope of its plant collections, and the distinction of its designed gardens, landscapes, and buildings. Since the 1890s, when this site was chosen for the Garden because of the beauty and diversity of its landscape, a pantheon of garden designers, architects, and landscape architects has collaborated within the strong framework of the natural features of the land to create the Garden as it is today. Beginning with the architect Calvert Vaux, the list of creators continues with such historic design figures as Samuel Parsons Jr., John R. Brinley, Beatrix Farrand, the Olmsted brothers, Ellen Shipman, Thomas H. Everett, and Marian Cruger Coffin.

In recent years, designers have included Dan Kiley, Penelope Hobhouse, Lynden B. Miller, Alice Ireys, Geoffrey Roesch, Jon Coe, Patrick Chassé, and Shavaun Towers. The work of these designers is revealed in the photographs and text of this book. Beginning with Lord & Burnham, the Garden has also always had fine architects, and they too are discussed in this book.

In addition to the visual qualities of the place, the Botanical Garden is also deservedly esteemed for the lofty goals of its scientific and educational mission and for more than a century of careful stewardship. When combined with its physical and intellectual position in the center of an illustrious city, these attributes make the New York Botanical Garden one of the world's most fascinating cultural institutions. No greater civic or urban amenity can be found—a museum of plants and an educational center housed within a landmark site of imperial proportions. It is not just an urban greensward, open-air classroom, major arboretum, or delightful array of display gardens; nor is it simply a place of respite and scholarship. It is none of these things alone, but all of them combined—the very definition of a classical botanical garden. Readers, be warned—you are entering enchanted territory!

WILSON NOLEN, *Chairman* GREGORY LONG, *President* THOMAS J. HUBBARD, *Chairman Emeritus*

Edward O. Wilson, Ph.D., the world-renowned biologist, is a Distinguished Counsellor to the board of the New York Botanical Garden. Among the many awards he has received for his influential work are the National Medal of Science and Pulitzer Prize. His quote is excerpted from remarks he made at the Botanical Garden in 2005.

PREVIOUS SPREAD
The ornamental cherry collection is strewn across the undulating hills of the Botanical Garden's nineteenth-century landscape.

OPPOSITE
The "Spring Flower Show" in the Conservatory features plants familiar to home gardeners. These foxgloves are among the thousands of flowers forced every year for Conservatory exhibitions by Garden horticulturists. The picturesque landscape of the site is framed by the building's historic windows.

Summa Altitudo aqua
Rhenolandiae Meridio
altitudo minima

Tabulae Ped. Rhenoland.

Virgae Rhenol.

HORTUS cum Sui
Aedificiis (ABCDEF
habet Virgas 200
et apparet Ocul
Supra Centrum (☉
elevato ad pedes 8.
ut Tabula docet
dimensus et depict
Aº 1718. industri
Nicolai Cruquii
Geometr

et Occidentis ab
in perpendiculum
turris academiae

G. Ingressus. H. horti pensiles ingressum ornantes.
1.2.3.4.5.6.7.8. Octo quadrae in quas area horti
divisa alit stirpes humi Consitas, cum Ambulacris
Spatiosis, Semitis, et Pulvinis in singulis quadris.
I. Pulvilli florum. J. Horti imaginarii Exoticarum.

O. hortus Adonid. alter magno Tepidario hypogaeo instructus.
P. horti Adonidis minores fenestris Vitreis et ligneis defensi.
Q. hortus Adonidis maximus fornace Calescens.
R. Pergula hybernaculum praebens Variis fornacib: instructum.
S. hybernaculum priore Calidius.

THE FIRST BOTANICAL GARDENS

A botanical garden contains documented, arranged collections of living plants for the various purposes of scientific research, conservation, cultivation, display, education, and enjoyment, often including a library, herbarium, arboretum, and greenhouses. A botanical garden is a modern version of Eden, an enclosed paradise where the geometry of designed flowerbeds and tree collections resides in reassuring harmony with Earth's natural shapes.

Although the great age of the botanical garden in Europe followed the discovery of the New World, the tradition began in the ancient world. Thousands of years before the Christian era, the Persians identified and cultivated plants exotic to their empire, which became the horticultural center of ancient times. In the third millennium B.C., Chinese emperor Shen Nung tested plant specimens that he collected for their medicinal properties. Tomb paintings at Thebes dated about 1500 B.C. reveal that the Egyptian royal gardens there contained fruit trees, grape arbors, waterlily pools, and herbaceous beds. In Classical Greece, the great philosopher Aristotle maintained a botanical garden in Athens and bequeathed it to his favorite pupil, Theophrastus, who eventually created the oldest-known descriptive botanical texts in the Western world.

The modern botanical garden, however, has its origins in the physic or medicinal gardens of medieval European monasteries, where monks ministered to the sick. The tradition that began in monastic gardens of cultivating orderly, hedge-bordered, and fenced plots of remedial herbs, each possessing its own property or curative virtue, led to the scientific and educational functions of later botanical gardens. The knowledge that grew out of these salutary practices was collected in herbals, first in manuscript form and eventually in books, after the advent of printing in the mid-fifteenth century. Herbals were the first textbooks of plant science, and the gardens of medicinal plants cultivated for and from them were the first true botanical gardens.

By the sixteenth century, the study of medicine had migrated to universities, where professors of medicine were primarily botanists. Because of the flow of new plants into Europe as a result of exploratory voyages to the Americas, Asia, and Africa, this was a rich period for the study of the world's flora. Cosimo I de' Medici founded the first "modern" science-based botanical garden of the University of Pisa in 1545, a garden that remains one of the glories of this renowned Italian city. Pisa was soon followed by the new botanical garden at Padua, also established as part of the medical school at the university. In 1590 the first scientific garden outside Italy was established in the Netherlands at the University of Leiden, which was a horticultural pioneer in greenhouse cultivation of the first plants brought into Europe from tropical and subtropical regions. By the turn of the seventeenth century, more than a thousand species and varieties were growing there, including six thousand South African Cape plants under glass. In 1735 twenty-eight-year-old Swedish botanist Carolus Linnaeus, whose work laid the foundation for modern plant science,

enrolled at the University of Leiden to further his studies in medicine; that year he published the first work on plant classification. Today Leiden, like Pisa, is still a working garden and a delight to visit.

Interest in botanical gardens crossed the channel to England in 1621, when Lord Henry Danvers put up the then-magnificent sum of five thousand pounds to establish a three-acre walled haven at Oxford, in the interest of having "a place whereby learning, especially the faculty of medicine, might be improved." More than half a century later, in 1673, the Chelsea Physic Garden was established near London, where it continues to occupy a charming, quiet corner of the city. There, a long line of famous British plantsmen, who collected plants and seeds from all over the world, created the idea of a botanical garden as a public museum and educational institution.

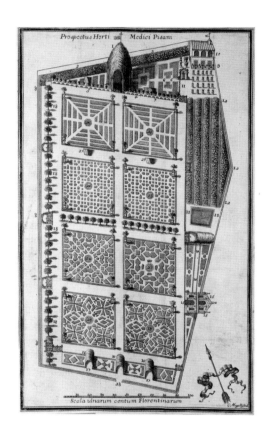

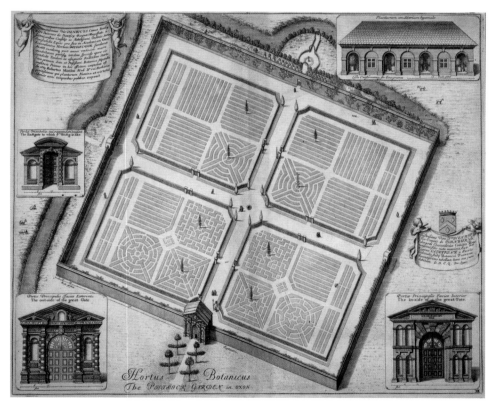

This hand-colored plate from a German edition of Elizabeth Blackwell's *Curious Herbal* reminds us of the intimate connections between early botanical gardens and the publications that documented their collections.

Vitis vinifera

1–11. Blüthe
12. Frucht
13.14. Saame

Wein-Stock.

King George III of England, a pastorally inclined monarch, maintained an extensive private pleasure garden at Kew in southwest London during the eighteenth century. In 1840 his garden became the public place known today as the Royal Botanic Gardens, Kew, a museum of living plants and a center for research, experiment, display, and delight. Eighteenth- and nineteenth-century British explorer-scientists Joseph Banks and William Jackson Hooker, with the sponsorship of the royal family, scoured the world for plants new to England and created a garden as famous then as now for its science, curiosities, and pleasures. During this period, public botanical gardens were also established in other European capital cities. A product of the age of exploration and a social movement aiming to provide urban dwellers with relief from city life, the modern botanical garden evolved into an ornamental landscape filled with exotic and beautiful plants maintained for educational and recreational purposes.

The famous Palm House at Kew, dating from the 1830s, inspired many imitations, none more significant than the Enid A. Haupt Conservatory at the New York Botanical Garden. *Reproduced with the kind permission of the Director and the Board of Trustees, Royal Botanic Gardens, Kew.*

CREATING A HAVEN FOR PEOPLE AND PLANTS

America, I believe, is the only country of consequence that does not possess an important botanical collection. . . . Surely the time is over-ripe for us to lay the foundations of such a collection as shall eclipse Kew itself and serve henceforth as a model to the world. . . . It behooves us in New York to be the first in the field, and to spare no pains to maintain the first place. . . . Here is an opportunity evidently vouchsafed by Providence in the nick of time. —Julian Hawthorne

In the summer of 1888, two young New Yorkers, Nathaniel Lord Britton and his new bride, Elizabeth Knight Britton, both of whom were serious botanists and academics, took a momentous trip to London. New Yorkers at this time were great admirers of British museums and other cultural institutions. The ruling class of financiers and industrialists in the Gilded Age looked to England and the Continent in the desire to found similar establishments that would civilize and dignify their American city, which had become a major world center. It is not surprising, therefore, that the Brittons, American tourists with a passion for plants, decided to visit the Royal Botanic Gardens, Kew, in London. They went for scientific reasons—to study medicinal plant specimens—but they were also enthralled by the fragrance and beauty of the "great domain" of Kew; drooping trees that brushed the quietly moving Thames; the distant sparkle of the Palm House dome; secluded gravel paths punctuated with welcoming rustic benches; "the matchless English turf, compact and flawless as velvet," studded with rhododendron beds.

Returning to New York, Elizabeth Britton gave impassioned speeches to promote the idea that the growing city needed a garden like Kew, and along the way, she started a civic movement. The *New York Herald* and other newspapers helpfully took up the banner: "Great Garden Needed; New York Should Have an Artistic Floral Study Ground; Laggards in Botany" and "Our Botanical Weakness; Awaiting the Leadership of a Citizen Who Would Embalm His Name in Flowers."

PREVIOUS SPREAD

When the great Conservatory was finished and opened to the public in 1902, it was an immediate sensation, as popular with schoolchildren as with adults and scholars.

ABOVE LEFT

The first governing board of the New York Botanical Garden included J. P. Morgan and Andrew Carnegie. The founding director, Nathaniel Lord Britton, is the fourth figure from the right. This photo was taken at the groundbreaking for the Library in December 1897.

ABOVE RIGHT

Some sections of the property were still farmed with horsepower when the New York Botanical Garden was given this site to manage in the late 1890s.

RIGHT

Rough yet picturesque countryside was cleared and groomed in the early days to create space for gardens and lawns.

The campaign was successful, and on April 28, 1891, the legislature of the State of New York passed an act incorporating the New York Botanical Garden and set aside 250 acres of undeveloped city-owned land in the northernmost part of the city "for the collection and culture of plants, flowers, shrubs and trees, [and] the advancement of botanical science and knowledge . . . and for the entertainment, recreation, and instruction of the people." At a meeting of the board of managers of the Botanical Garden on June 18, 1895, the "fully subscribed" completion of the initial endowment mandate of $250,000 was proudly announced, including major contributions by some of the most prominent and influential citizens of the day, including Andrew Carnegie, J. P. Morgan, John D. Rockefeller, and Cornelius Vanderbilt. In May of 1896, Nathaniel Lord Britton, having left his professorship at Columbia University, was named director in chief by board president Vanderbilt.

Planning for the Botanical Garden was begun under the direction of Calvert Vaux, co-designer of Central Park with Frederick Law Olmsted. After his untimely death in 1895, the Brittons and their colleagues, Samuel Parsons Jr. and John R. Brinley, took over landscaping and architectural decisions. The concept was that a portion of the acreage would be preserved intact, including a first-growth stand of forest along the Bronx River; the garden displays themselves would be situated in the meadows to the west; and the plantings and the rock garden would follow a "natural treatment." By the spring of 1897, the herbaceous plantings included more than fifteen hundred species.

Following the advice of officials at Kew, the larger buildings—the Library and the great Conservatory—would be situated far apart, in anticipation of weekend crowds. On New Year's Eve in 1897, ground was broken on a hill to the east of the railroad station for the Library, a three-hundred-foot-long, six-story limestone structure in the Italian Renaissance style, graced by Corinthian pilasters and a dome. The contract for the glass, cast-iron, steel, and swamp cypress Conservatory was awarded in 1897 to the firm of Lord & Burnham, preeminent designers and builders of customized curvilinear greenhouses for the American aristocracy. Completed in 1902, the Garden's crystal palace featured a ninety-foot-high central Palm Court with eleven interconnected greenhouses arranged in a symmetrical, rectilinear "C" shape.

Although her husband was a hands-on manager from the outset and very much in charge, Elizabeth Britton also put an enduring personal stamp on the Garden. She was a devoted

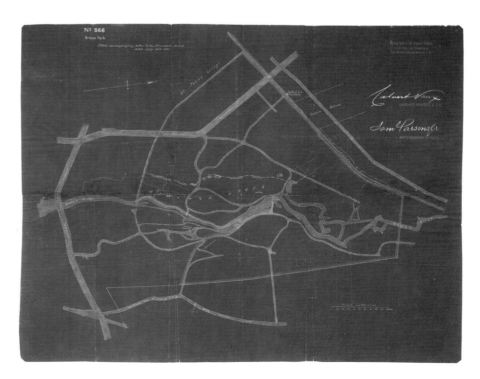

An early plan of the Botanical Garden's roadways and paths designed by Calvert Vaux. Vaux worked on the Garden's layout in the mid-1890s.

volunteer, graciously hosting teatime meetings to promote its mission. In addition to spending many hours a day conducting research, studying, and cataloguing the impressive new collection of moss specimens, which she published widely, she inaugurated a national lecture campaign in 1902 to increase public awareness of wildflower preservation. That same year, the Brittons began their botanical excursions to the Caribbean and the West Indies to investigate tropical flora.

In concert with the twin imperatives of horticultural display and ongoing research, education was of paramount importance to the founders, and it has been so ever since. Whereas botanical gardens had first been established for the collection and propagation of medicinal plants and, after the Renaissance, for the promotion of scientific exploration and the study of the plants of the world's flora, now, in modern America, such institutions were expanded to include horticultural display, gardening, and the education of the citizenry. The most significant contribution made by Americans to the concept of botanical gardens is that they have become, above all, educational institutions. The Brittons created lecture programs for the public, and school groups came to learn plant science and to see plants of the world. By 1910 more than twenty thousand children from all over the city took part each year in these lectures and practical demonstrations.

Throughout the many generations since the 1890s, the leadership of the New York Botanical Garden has remained dedicated to its original mission. Today one hundred thousand New York City-area schoolchildren visit the Garden every year, and new facilities such as the Everett Children's Adventure Garden, designed in the 1990s for the study of plants and nature, have been created to serve them. The great Victorian-style Conservatory, which almost fell to the ground in the 1970s but is now restored and run by computers and expert horticulturists, houses a major annual rotation of changing plant and flower shows and presents beautiful and informative exhibitions about the plants of the world—their ecology and conservation, and the importance of research.

These are not the only changes, however. An entire century of development and stewardship has resulted in a carefully tended historic

Many New York City children have grown up learning to enjoy nature in the idyllic setting of the Botanical Garden.

landscape and in many new facilities, in which thousands of classes, public programs, and informal sessions help an ever-increasing audience learn about plants, gardening, nature, and science.

By the early twenty-first century, more than two thousand scientific expeditions had been sent throughout the world and hundreds of students had received their Ph.D.s through the Garden's graduate program. Although molecular biology has now entered the scene and somewhat changed the methodology, the scientific questions remain the same: What is the evolutionary history of the plants on Earth; how can they be of use to mankind when we know more about them; and how can we promote plant conservation worldwide?

This book documents what a treasured American and international institution the Brittons' dream child has become. Readers will discover the gardens and the collections of this romantic place with its picturesque, rolling, rocky, forested, and lake-strewn landscape, where it can truly be said that the Hudson Valley begins.

Julian Hawthorne was the son of the American novelist Nathaniel Hawthorne. His quote is excerpted from "An American Kew," which was published in Lippincotts Magazine *(January 1891).*

The Library building, a grand Beaux-Arts edifice, was designed by Robert Gibson. This photo was taken in 1901.

THE GARDEN TODAY

A SPLENDID NATURAL SITE   KIM E. TRIPP

The great Hudson River sweeps through its grand valley along the entire eastern border of New York State, finally reaching the Atlantic Ocean through the landscapes and harbors of New York City. As the river nears the ocean, the mainland reaches "land's end" in the New York borough of the Bronx. This landscape of stone outcrops and rolling terrain was created by the glaciers that once carved and covered the rocky land and by the humans who crafted a balance of forest, farm, pond, and meadow from the earliest days of their wanderings and settlements.

This remarkable region has been an important haven for people since prehistory. Today, at its northern edge, the river, lakes, forest, gardens, and historic architecture of the New York Botanical Garden constitute a National Historic Landmark of 250 acres. Since 1895, this splendid site has benefited from constant stewardship, which has preserved its unique natural and designed features for the public. The original plan for the Garden called for no earth moving, no relocation of huge rocks, no digging of valleys, no building of lakes and ponds. There was no need for these alterations; the natural landscape was picturesque enough. Knolls and dales are laid over and around the rock where soil and plants make a soft cover. The freshwater Bronx River flows through the Garden from north to south on its way from Westchester County to the East River, creating a dramatic gorge through the rock. Other small streams and seasonal brooks sparkle and tumble through the Garden's landscape, which is dotted with several ponds and lakes. It was all there—a natural setting for the anticipated plant collections and ornamental gardens of New York's grand new botanical garden.

In the center of the Garden, wrapping both sides of the Bronx River, lies the largest remaining tract of native northeastern forest in New York City. This fifty-acre forest is famous for its venerable native trees, such as oak, sweetgum, maple, and tulip tree. The forest was admired and preserved by members of the Lorillard family, who settled the area in the late eighteenth century. The city acquired part of their estate after the passage of the New Parks Act in 1884 and set aside 250 acres for the Botanical Garden, which was established here in 1895.

Today Garden visitors are drawn to the forest's woodland, dramatic views, and array of native birds, including both permanent residents and migratory species. Great horned owls, Cooper's hawks, rare warblers, ibis, and, on the river itself, mergansers and wood ducks are among the interesting birds that visitors find. The trees in the forest range in age from young saplings to mature specimens hundreds of years old. The Garden manages the forest using an innovative plan that permits nature to take its course throughout much of the forest, allowing for trees to decay and return their nutrients to the soil. In certain areas, where exotic species are competing with the native plants and where trails are maintained so that visitors and researchers can walk into the area and experience its diversity with minimal impact, the forest is more intensively managed to help insure its future integrity and vigor. Mature trees native to the site also grow outside the forest throughout the Garden's historic grounds.

The original plan and carriageways through the Garden were laid out by architect Calvert Vaux in 1894. He designed the routes in lovely, simple, winding ways around the rock outcrops, hills, dells, and forest; these carriageways called for stone bridges to be built over the river and the

lakes; and they dictated clear and logical locations for the future development of gardens and buildings. The Vaux plan was developed and formalized by the Olmsted brothers master plan of the 1920s.

More than a century after its founding in this landscape, the Garden is now embroidered with an extensive set of designed gardens, plant collections, and flower borders. Fifty gardens and plant collections nestle within the site, and a suite of historic and modern buildings serves the Garden's work as a museum and laboratory for plants. The venerable wild-collected conifer species of northern and boreal forests are grown and displayed in the Arthur and Janet Ross Conifer Arboretum, the first collection established at the Garden, which greets visitors as they enter the main gate. Walking through the landscape, one comes upon the magnolia, lilac, cherry, or crabapple collections covered in glorious clouds of flower, complementing the formal Peggy Rockefeller Rose Garden, filled with thousands of roses; the Jane Watson Irwin Perennial Garden richly planted with flowers three seasons of the year; and the Benenson Ornamental Conifers collection with its fantastic display of hundreds of dwarf and specialty conifers that delight and inspire all year round. Carefully tended and environmentally sensitive lawns create a soft, green background for the mature trees and gardens.

The natural site of the New York Botanical Garden is a unique treasure preserved in perpetuity for the public and for professional horticulturists and botanists alike. It is the setting for now extensive plant collections and provides one of the most exciting landscapes possessed by any botanical garden in the world.

The gardens and flower borders of the New York Botanical Garden have been designed and developed since 1895, creating a seasonal tapestry of flowers, fragrance, fruit, and foliage. These gardens also display a vast range of horticultural styles, from the most traditional and historic to the most innovative and experimental, and they show more than one million garden plants in varied combinations and garden settings.

Experiencing this horticultural array can be as cozy as an afternoon stroll to the intimate Rock Garden to see if the hardy orchids have begun to flower or as spectacular as a visit to the Peggy Rockefeller Rose Garden in June, when thousands of different roses in full flower create a swelling of rose blossoms.

Each season brings a different set of horticultural pleasures. In spring, waves of daffodils, carpets of alpines, sweeps of early bulbs, new perennials, and ephemeral peonies make their appearance. In summer, daylilies, woodland shade perennials, bamboos, and borders of tropical plants offer bold and lush color and form. In fall, asters, chrysanthemums, late anemones, spires of blue monk's hood, waving grasses, and autumn crocus sparkle with color in harmony with the turning foliage of the trees. In winter, camellias, hellebores, witch-hazels, Japanese flowering apricots, mahonia, and a host of other unusual plants bring color and fragrance to the snowy landscape.

JANE WATSON IRWIN PERENNIAL GARDEN

This Perennial Garden is a blend of herbaceous perennials with ornamental grasses, bulbs, seasonal annuals, shrubs, and small trees, interplanted to create texture, color, and fragrance throughout the year. The garden was designed and developed as a mixed border—that is, one including all types of ornamental plants—by Lynden B. Miller, a plantswoman and garden designer renowned for her striking use of plant combinations in designs created especially for public gardens.

The Perennial Garden is arranged in a series of garden "rooms" that recollects the garden-design concept perfected by English gardeners such as Vita Sackville-West at Sissinghurst Castle in Kent. The New York Botanical Garden Perennial Garden rooms are defined by season and color. A visit usually begins in the fall room, where herbaceous perennials and shrubs combine to offer peak color and texture during the autumn. The bronze tones of ornamental grasses, the burgundy leaves of Japanese maples, and the surprising *Amsonia hubrichtii*—a feathery textured, native perennial that turns burnished gold in October—are enlivened by the colors of late-flowering salvias from Mexico and color selections of Korean chrysanthemums. Professional horticulturists and casual home gardeners alike discover these fall flowers as interesting new choices for autumn gardens throughout the region.

PREVIOUS SPREAD

Herbaceous peonies die to the ground annually, but the larger and even more magnificent Chinese tree peonies, such as those shown in this photo, grow on woody stems like small shrubs.

RIGHT

The deep, mixed perennial borders designed by Lynden B. Miller are ravishing from late summer until Thanksgiving in many years.

OPPOSITE

The Perennial Garden, originally laid out by American landscape architect Dan Kiley, is composed of many "rooms."

OPPOSITE

The idea behind the New York Botanical Garden's herbaceous plantings is that they should be as fine as those found in the most luxurious private gardens.

LEFT

An ornamental grapevine suns itself on an armillary sphere.

BELOW LEFT

Spring brings poppies, bulbs, and flowering trees.

33

OPPOSITE
The Perennial Garden unfolds
in room after room as one's eye
moves across to the dome of
the Conservatory.

ABOVE LEFT
Biennial *Eryngium giganteum*,
known in England as "Miss
Willmott's ghost," is allowed to
self sow, here effectively inter-
twining with an annual ageratum.

LEFT
Sometimes tropical plants such as
this red cordyline are set out in the
summer among hardy perennials
and shrubs.

ABOVE
Oriental hybrid lilies spread
a strong perfume across
the Perennial Garden on hot
summer afternoons.

Red crocosmia and blue balloon flower are happy partners. They seem not to know they are living in the middle of New York City.

The visitor next reaches the bog room, which is planted with a combination of northeastern native plants that are well adapted to wet conditions and offer showy flowers, foliage, or fruit combined with ornamental plants of diverse origin. For example, in summer, red, blue, and purple lobelias are combined with the delicate ruby pincushions of *Astrantia* and graceful variegated iris.

The next area is the hot room, ablaze with color throughout the spring, summer, and fall. Here the orange-and-cream flowers of red-hot poker spear through the smoky-purple cloud of bronze fennel foliage and give the nod to the burgundy-red leaves of the *Canna* 'King Humbert' (which must be taken in for the winter each year). Shrubs such as sand cherry (*Prunus × cistena*) keep their cherry-red foliage throughout the season and mix brilliantly with gold-foliaged dwarf conifers; combinations of bright new annuals, such as *Salvia* 'Blue Chiquita', enrich each season. The hot room is also home to plantings of daylilies selected from the Garden's historic collection of rare varieties developed by Dr. Arlow Stout in the mid-twentieth century. Dr. Stout maintained an important breeding program at the Garden, developing entirely new colors and forms of daylilies.

After the brightness of the hot room, strolling into the cool room of the Perennial Garden is a visual experience akin to a refreshing dip in a pristine lake on a hot, sunny day. In this room, pastel shrub roses keep close company with spikes of purple monk's-hood flowers and dark evergreen dwarf conifers. This refreshing palette is expressed in foliage plants as well. A mosaic of hostas, ferns, and shade-loving ornamental grasses is a cushion for pink and white Japanese anemones from late summer to fall, and for bulbs such as crocuses, fritillaries, and camassias in spring. The design of the Perennial Garden relies on the height of evergreen shrubs and the rhythmic repetition of color and form to create an underlying harmony among all the plants.

A long view in the Perennial Garden reveals its inspiration in the great flower borders of Edwardian England.

These brilliant botanical illustrations reflect the beauty of flowers in the Perennial Garden as well as in the Library: *Aquilegia* (right), *Monarda* (opposite left), and *Campanula* (opposite right).

W.G.Smith,F.L.S.del et lith.

AQUILEGIA CHRYSANTHA,
(Aquilegia leptocera. var. lutea.)

V.Brooks,Day&Son.Imp.

FLORAL MAGAZINE. NEW SERIES.
L.Reeve &Co.5,Henrietta. St.Covent Garden.

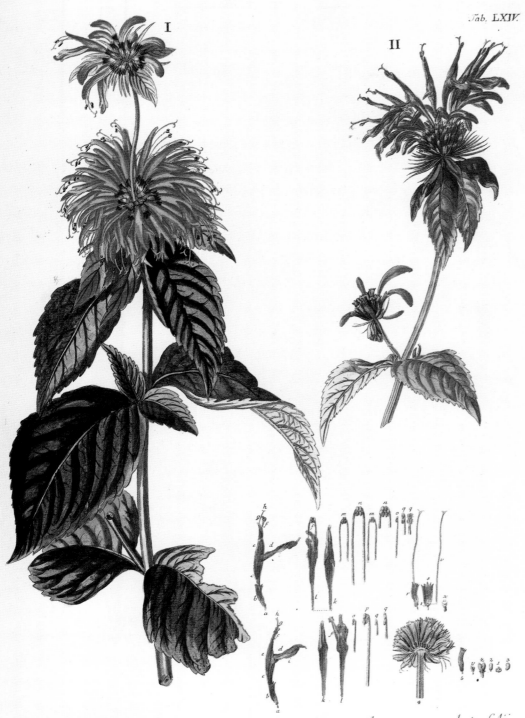

Tab. LXIV.

MONARDA *floribus capitatis et verticillatis, caule acute angulato, foliis lanceolatis serratis glabris Buttn. enumer. plant. Hort. Cliff. 226.*

a.a. flos separatus, b.b. ejus calyx, c.c. corolla tubus, d.d. limbus ringens, e.e. labium superius erectum, f.f.f.f. duo stamina, g.g. stylus, h.h. ejus stigma bifurcatum, i.i. labium inferius reflexum, k.k. labium superius separatum a facie interiore, l.l. labium inferius separatum trifidum a facie interiore, m.m. ambo stamina a tubo separata cum antheris in magnitudine naturali, n.n. aucta, o.o. stamen cum anthera in magnitudine naturali, p.aucta, q.q.q.q. cum antheris hiantibus, r. calyx separatus cum stylo, s.idem calyx verticaliter dissectus cum quinque denticulis, t. ovarium, v.stylus separatus, ta, q.q.q.q. cum antheris hiantibus, r. calyx separatus cum stylo, s. idem calyx verticaliter dissectus cum quinque denticulis, t. ovarium, v. stylus separatus tus, x. ovarium separatum, y. quatuor ovarii semina in magnitudine naturali, z. aucta, 1. transverse dissecta, 2. semen perfectum a facie exteriore, 3. interiore, 4. verticillus calycum persistentium, 5. ejusmodi calyx separatus.

Campanule gantelée.   *Campanula*

P. J. Redouté.   *Langlois.*

NANCY BRYAN LUCE HERB GARDEN

Next to the Perennial Garden is a semiformal, brick-walled garden designed in the tradition of herb and knot gardens. Interpreted with an historic slant by Penelope Hobhouse in the 1990s, the Herb Garden was originally created in the 1940s to display and grow herbs and companion plants with an emphasis on American species and native traditions. A central boxwood parterre frames a set of beds for changing seasonal plantings—ornamental and fragrant basils and sages make their appearance here, along with ornamental onions. Borders contain permanent plantings of curative, culinary, or fragrant herbs and companion plants and shrubs.

OPPOSITE
Boxwood knots in the Herb Garden lie at the foot of hills covered with magnificent specimen trees.

LEFT
As a matter of tradition, the "H" in Herb Garden is pronounced at the New York Botanical Garden. An opinionated lady who was a volunteer long ago dictated, "If this is an 'erb garden, well, the 'ell with it."

In some seasons, a set of terra-cotta containers is often placed in a formal pattern within the Herb Garden to allow for the display of herbs and flowers, often the newest varieties of ornamental and culinary herbs. Tree basil and rosemary standards are often used, underplanted with variegated thymes, as are unexpected combinations of fern-leaf dill and parsley mixed with pastel fragrant herbs, such as stocks or sweet peas.

Flanking the entrance to the Herb Garden is a pair of Silver Frost flowering pears that are lightly sheared—in keeping with the semiformal character of the garden—into soft globes. These trees are covered with white flowers in spring and then turn to silver spheres in the summer as the trees leaf out with slender, silver foliage. These elegant pears make a perfect gateway and enticing entrance for garden lovers.

Americans who love gardening
and the outdoors know that
winter is a time to be treasured in
the garden.

LADIES' BORDER

The Ladies' Border is a long, deep bed of bulbs, herbaceous perennials, grasses, ferns, shrubs, and trees that parades along a walkway at the southern end of the Enid A. Haupt Conservatory. Originally created by designer Ellen Biddle Shipman in the 1930s, this border was established as a gardener's model, one of the first grand flower borders in New York City. At the time Shipman designed it, the idea of a broad flowering border "painted" with a changing palette of plants was an innovation. It was created on a large scale—260 feet long and 20 feet deep. Shipman's original plans, which are archived in the Garden's LuEsther T. Mertz Library, show the border as intricately designed with many layers of mixed plantings.

The creation of the border was supported by a group of volunteer women who had a great interest in gardens and all things horticultural. The group made possible this major addition to the Garden's array of plantings and gardens, hence the name "Ladies' Border." By 2000, however, the border was in need of significant restoration and refreshment. Garden designer Lynden B. Miller and the Garden staff were inspired to restore the border to its original glory in keeping with Shipman's original spirit of innovation.

Therefore, Miller developed a plan that would re-create a mixed border in Shipman's style but would rely on a new and modern plant palette, bravely expanded to include many half-hardy and Mediterranean plants that might become part of the regular plant palette in New York given the gradual warming of the climate in this area. The concept was for the Ladies' Border to become a showcase and proving ground for new plants as well as plants from heretofore untried climates. Renowned colleagues in the plant world were consulted to find the most intriguing plants, and the result is a horticultural tour de force. New crape-myrtles, camellias, mahonia, *Adonis, Edgeworthia*, and Japanese flowering apricot are just a few of the plants that have thrived in the border.

This crape-myrtle flowers profusely in the Ladies' Border. Only a few years ago, these shrubs were not considered hardy in the New York City region.

SEASONAL WALK

Among the Garden's set of large flower borders, this border along Seasonal Walk is perhaps the most extravagant. One of only a few such examples remaining in public gardens throughout the world, this border, in keeping with the late-Victorian tradition, is completely replanted four times a year to create entirely fresh and dramatic horticultural displays. At 184 feet long and 10 feet wide, this border poses a challenge that can be accomplished only by the most expert horticultural staff. The Garden's curators and gardeners make horticultural theater of their work in this expansive border.

"Act One" is an intricate sea of tulips that stretches the length of the border in May. Each year the tulips are totally replanted with a new design incorporating fresh bulbs, which insures the tulips' vigor in flowering and the visitors' interest in viewing the border annually. The second act is a fresh carpet of spring biennials, perennials, and annuals, all planted into a finished border design at flowering stage—a bit of horticultural magic that requires perfect timing so the different spring plants flower at the same time. The third act is a set of summer scenes created with tropical plants, ferns, vines, and ground-cover plants selected for colorful flowers or foliage or for their bold texture. Some of the most exotic plants appear in this summer show, which culminates in an autumn finale of Swiss chard, kale, cabbages, and the horticultural queens of the fall garden, chrysanthemums, always in a new mix of colors and textures.

OPPOSITE
A major tulip planting is a luxury since it must be dug up and replanted annually.

RIGHT
This elegant botanical plate featuring an antique King Frederick tulip captures the beauty of the thousands of tulips seen each spring along Seasonal Walk.

HOME GARDENING CENTER

Home gardeners are always in search of the best plants and the most accurate tips on how to plant, sow, grow, control pests, fertilize, compost, garden in winter, deal with climate change and watering, prune, have fun, learn as much as possible, grow the greatest plants and, in general, get the most out of their gardens. Whether those gardens are a few pots on a windowsill, an urban courtyard, a backyard vegetable garden, or an extensive array of formal gardens and country borders, the questions remain the same.

The purpose of the New York Botanical Garden's Home Gardening Center is to supply information and ideas for every type of garden. Designed to reflect the scale of the home garden, the center includes plant and lawn trials, which show the best varieties of garden plants and lawn grasses for home gardens. It is also the venue for seasonal gardening workshops and demonstrations held on weekends in the Kenneth Roman Gazebo and in the gardens themselves.

A walk through the Home Gardening Center shows the visitor every aspect of gardening. The first stop is the Plant Trials Garden, which comprises more than five thousand square feet of plantings that feature the best varieties for home gardens. Next is a series of demonstration gardens with various themes, such as Helen's Garden of Fragrant Plants, which presents an extensive array of fragrant flower and foliage plants. Designed in the 1980s by Alice Ireys, the Mae L. Wien Cutting Garden showcases flowers, foliage, and even beautiful stems for cut-flower

OPPOSITE

The Home Gardening Center includes an expansive Plant Trials Garden created not for specialists or growers but for visitors who want new ideas for their own backyards.

FAR LEFT

One of the many tips offered in the Home Gardening Center demonstrations is how to create attractive container plantings.

LEFT

A specimen from the Garden's research collections illustrates the seeds of a grass similar to the ornamental grasses grown around the Kenneth Roman Gazebo in the Home Gardening Center.

arrangements, with tips on the best methods for cutting and preserving flowers. The Louise Loeb Vegetable Garden demonstrates innovative ways to grow vegetables, herbs, and companion flowers year round, including the use of portable, homemade cold frames to give gardeners an early start in spring and to grow hardy vegetables to enliven the table during the winter. The Compost Demonstration shows a variety of composting techniques, including commercially available composters. The Korean Chrysanthemum Garden is a unique border of hundreds of hardy chrysanthemums that are grown as perennials and make a fantastic showing every autumn. Recently refurbished by garden designer Patrick Chassé, the Rodney White Country Garden is a vignette of great garden plants, especially those for shady gardens, drawn from the traditional American palette of country gardens. Its layers of flowering trees, shrubs, perennials, ferns, foliage plants, and bulbs are full of irresistible ideas to try at home.

Late-flowering Korean chrysanthemums, raised every year from seed and cuttings, provide remarkable color in November.

DAYLILY/DAFFODIL WALK

The gracefully curving walk from the Mertz Library to the Haupt Conservatory is lined with borders that combine hundreds of daffodils with hundreds of daylilies to create a tapestry of floral display from early spring through mid summer. The Daylily/Daffodil Walk is bordered by eight long beds that are filled with daffodils in early spring. As the daffodils recede, daylilies emerge from among them to grow and flower brightly through the summer, creating a new floral display from the same planting bed. The daffodil bulbs and the daylily crowns are planted into alternative spaces in the border, a creative approach to interplanting that insures two great flowering shows for the use of one border area—an idea applicable to home gardens.

The daylily collection is arranged like a colorful ribbon that winds through the Ross Conifer Arboretum.

The daffodils grown along Daylily/Daffodil Walk are all varieties that have proven to be reliable and handsome selections grown in the Garden's more formal narcissus collections. They represent a selection from all the various horticultural types, with an emphasis on those commercially available to all gardeners. The varieties are labeled so that visitors may make notes of newly discovered favorites in order to seek out the same plants at a local nursery.

Eleanor Clarke

In early spring, just as New Yorkers are at their wits' end with the winter browns, leftover snow and ice, the cold, the dark, and the absence of all things floriferous, daffodils appear in drifts and bursts—and in the most cheerful colors and presentations. Trumpets and petticoats of yellow, cream, pink, silver, tangerine, and golden orange are all lifted from a cheerful green swath of leaves, a sure sign that spring has arrived.

There is no better place to be cheered by daffodils than at the New York Botanical Garden's narcissus collection, which is planted throughout the valley east of the Rock Garden, along the forest's edge. More than fifty thousand daffodils are planted there, arranged by the thirteen horticultural classes that categorize the types of daffodil from Division I: Trumpet to Division XIII: Species types. More than two hundred varieties are currently grown and displayed each year, and the collection is regularly enhanced with new varieties from the different classes.

The daffodils are labeled every spring, so that a stroll among them reveals their names and types. This is the most diverse and extensive collection of daffodil varieties in any public garden in America, which means that a visit to this collection is an opportunity to not only enjoy one of the most beautiful gardens anywhere, but also to learn about and select varieties to grow yourself.

How do the curators keep track of all of these plants? The Garden organizes its plant collections in a sophisticated, computer-based mapping system that is linked to a database used by the curators to record the Garden's living plant collections. Each spring, the staff surveys the daffodil collection plantings for location and variety—a task that must be completed while they are all still in flower in order to verify the types.

OPPOSITE
The daffodil collections appear to be painted on the turf of the Garden's natural landscape.

RIGHT
The daffodil collection is arranged in immense pools of single varieties, all labeled to provide a living encyclopedia.

ABOVE
Daffodils in the lawn with weeping cherries against a watery sky—sometimes New York looks like England.

OPPOSITE
The Liasson Narcissus Collection carpets a valley beneath the hills of the first-growth forest.

ROCK GARDEN

The Rock Garden is a two-and-one-half-acre gem tucked against the northwestern edge of the native forest. It is framed by a tall curtain of mature trees, such as oak, maple, and sweetgum, on the forest edge, by blue Atlas cedars sweeping over from the Ross Conifer Arboretum, and by flowering cherries near the entrance. The garden was conceived as a blend of traditional alpine garden rockeries with woodland stream and shade gardens, all accompanied by choice perennials. This unique combination makes a glorious garden indeed.

This is a very intimate, quiet garden, set away from the busy walks in the Garden's general landscape. A sparkling waterfall and stream flow into a woodland pond, and a shaded path traverses the stream over a bit of rock bridge before winding along past the waterfall and the Rock Garden's plantings. The traditional rock or alpine garden grew out of an idea created in nineteenth-century Europe as a way to bring the experience of climbing high alpine paths and meadows down into the gardens and estates of lower elevations. The first alpine gardens were made by piling rocks in concentrated areas to create good drainage and mimic the alpine environment, and then by planting alpine and companion plants within these rockeries.

ABOVE LEFT
When the Rock Garden was built, the natural outcroppings on the site were augmented by stones moved in from other sections of the landscape.

ABOVE
Although the Rock Garden was built in the 1930s, age-old and laborious techniques of moving rock were utilized.

OPPOSITE
The Rock Garden is home to thousands of alpine plants and fine trees and shrubs, including the *Rhododendron keiskei* seen here in the foreground.

Massive oaks provide perimeter shade and shelter for the secluded valley of the Rock Garden.

The Rock Garden has grown out of this tradition and incorporates many historical elements. It was originally conceived and built on its current site by the Garden's renowned horticulturist Thomas H. Everett in the 1930s. This is one of only two areas in the Garden where rock was placed and manipulated to create the landscape (the other is the Benenson Ornamental Conifers). Except for the high rock outcrop behind the waterfall—a natural feature of the forest edge—almost all the rocks were set by men and women, who used horses and simple equipment. (Much of the labor force was provided by the Works Progress Administration, created by President Franklin Roosevelt in 1935, during the Great Depression.) Everett planned the garden to display a sequence of views and alpine habitats, as well as beautiful woodland and meadow areas and the waterfall, stream, and pond.

A gentian collected from Soviet Georgia in the Western Caucasus, here displayed in a dried specimen, is not very different from the living gentians seen by visitors to the Rock Garden.

The brilliant blue of gentian is as sparkling in this botanical illustration as it is in the living plant.

Rare gentians from the Western Caucasus are Rock Garden favorites.

OPPOSITE
The pond in spring is bordered
by a luxuriant planting of
leucojum and marsh-marigolds—
a combination easily replicated
by the home gardener.

LEFT
A long view down the Rock
Garden toward the Native Plant
Garden

Today there are new features as well. At the entrance is a set of specially created troughs (small, deep, masonry planters reminiscent of old watering troughs at stables and inns), which show rare miniature alpines that flower throughout the season. Tiny pincushions of saxifrage, diminutive alpine iris and columbine, and rare gentians with their cerulean-blue trumpets of flowers are cushioned in these jewel-box planters. The troughs are set into a carpet of choice woodland ephemerals, including a variety of wild-gingers.

The pond and its streamside plantings are the next area to come into view. Shaded by an ancient Japanese hemlock, whose graceful branches brush the surface of the water, these gardens feature a wonderful palette of shade and woodland herbaceous perennials, ferns, and bulbs. At certain

RIGHT
Ferns, hostas, ancient rocks, and splashing water

FAR RIGHT
This columbine specimen in the Herbarium is a close relative of many of the columbines grown in the Rock Garden.

OPPOSITE
Fresh spring growth on an overhanging hemlock frames a view of the pond.

times, the Japanese primroses shine in a ribbon from the moist stream bed and pond edges—their candelabras of pinks, yellows, cherry-reds, and lavenders creating a stream of colors in their own right.

While crossing the rock bridge, one has a long view down the length of the garden and its meadow, and around the curve of the path one can glimpse hardy orchids in flower. It seems impossible that these large, fragile flowers could be perennial plants in the northern garden, but indeed they are. Other choice woodland plants from around the world emerge from this shaded dell, some quite large; *Cardiocrinum giganteum*,

RIGHT
The delicate tracery of the fruits, flowers, and foliage of pasque flower are preserved forever in the pressed plants of the Herbarium collection.

OPPOSITE
The small, cheerful pasque flower is known as such because it often blooms at Easter time.

the giant Himalayan lily from China, reaches six to ten feet in height and is crowned by a tiara of huge lily blossoms with purple centers—a truly remarkable sight.

Further along the path, water emerges from the depths of the native forest and a waterfall descends musically down among the rock and gravel run of the cascade garden, which is strewn with naturalized alpine flowers—pasque flower, miniature bell flower, aubrietia, even alpine tulips. Next to the waterfall is one of the oldest known trees in the Garden, a 250-year-old black oak (*Quercus velutina*), a longstanding sentinel at the edge of the forest.

Other habitats here include the alpine scree, with its delicate *Lewisia;* montane dryland, with high-elevation agave and flowering cactus; the crevice garden, with tiny alpines, including *Fumana* and *Vitaliana* from the mountains of Europe, near a carpet of hardy cyclamen; the moist moraine plain; and the alpine meadow with carpets of creeping phlox. Each setting displays a unique set of plants, some of which can be grown by the home gardener, but most of which demand an advanced level of horticultural skill and commitment, a fact that makes the pleasure of visiting the Rock Garden even more stimulating. This is an experience that cannot be replicated at home or found in any other public garden in America.

This specimen used for
illustration ed 3
Britton & Brown's Flora

New York
Botanical
Garden

Dryopteris austriaca var. dilatata

Herbarium of the New York Botanical Garden

Dryopteris dilatata (Hoffm.) Gray
The Gorge, near Bald Peak, Rutland Co. 68.
H.S. Ross & M. Sloan   Sept. 1910
alt. about 1400 ft.

OPPOSITE

A hosta species from Japan with
bold leaves and handsome flowers
thrives beside the Rock Garden
cascade.

LEFT

The fern shown here in a specimen
from the Garden's Herbarium can
also be found in the Rock Garden.

NATIVE PLANT GARDEN

Native plants have become a popular theme in modern gardening. The focus on environmentally sound horticulture, local resources, and the understanding of ecology and conservation has led to a new regard for native plants. At the New York Botanical Garden, "native" is a term that refers to plants indigenous to the northeastern United States. Some of the plants grown here are American natives endangered in the wild; these are grown as part of a national conservation effort coordinated by the Center for Plant Conservation, of which the Botanical Garden is a founding participant.

The Native Plant Garden is arranged around the natural features of the landscape. The forest stretches along the edge of the garden, where tall native trees create a shady canopy and an opportunity to display ephemeral native woodland wildflowers, such as trillium, diverse ferns, and native woodland flowering shrubs.

The meandering stream that begins its course in the Rock Garden flows through the Native Plant Garden before spreading into the wetland next to the Everett Children's Adventure Garden. The stream makes it possible to grow a wetland meadow border of native wildflowers and grasses. This graceful naturalized border matures in summer, when bold plants such as the swamp mallow with its tall stems, bold leaves, and saucer-sized red and pink flowers make a dramatic garden feature.

RIGHT
This trillium specimen from the Herbarium is closely related to species enjoyed by visitors to the Native Plant Garden.

OPPOSITE
Massive rock outcroppings native to the site provide mossy crevices used to display native American plants.

ABOVE

Early spring brings false-hellebore
up on the floor of the woods in the
Native Plant Garden. This plant,
not often used by American
gardeners, is easy to grow and
highly recommended.

RIGHT

This lovely botanical illustration
shows *Helonias bullata*, the swamp
pink. Living specimens of this rare
plant can be seen in the Native
Plant Garden.

CIMICIFUGA RACEMOSA.

Plate III.

Uvularia Perfoliata   Uvulaire Perfoliée

These beautifully preserved plates illustrate two wonderful native plants for gardeners in the north-east: white-flowered black cohosh (left) and yellow-flowered bellwort (above).

PEGGY ROCKEFELLER ROSE GARDEN

The rose, which has been in cultivation for centuries as a medicinal, ornamental, and commercial plant, has inspired and informed all aspects of human endeavor from war to poetry. It is America's national flower.

Therefore, it seems appropriate that one of the most magnificent views at the New York Botanical Garden is down into the valley of the Peggy Rockefeller Rose Garden, especially in June and September, when the roses are in full flower. The roses fill the ancient lake bed that is the setting for this garden with their own pool of color, and on a warm day, their fragrance rises up to compete with the view as the most beautiful aspect of this site.

The Rose Garden has an interesting history. The landscape architect Beatrix Jones Farrand created the ingenious triangular plan for this site in 1916. Her formal yet visually arresting idea for the garden was likely inspired by the French tradition of formal Rose Gardens. She used an asymmetrical triangle as the outline; the central focus was a formal gazebo with paths radiating outward and rose beds laid out at angles from the walks. The garden is surrounded by a tall lattice fence that serves as support for the climbing roses that range around the perimeter. Also in the perimeter beds are the old-fashioned shrub roses, which predate modern roses. Here is where the harlequin 'Rosa Mundi' and its relatives can be

Original blueprints for the Peggy Rockefeller Rose Garden, designed by Beatrix Jones Farrand, are housed in the Garden's extensive archives.

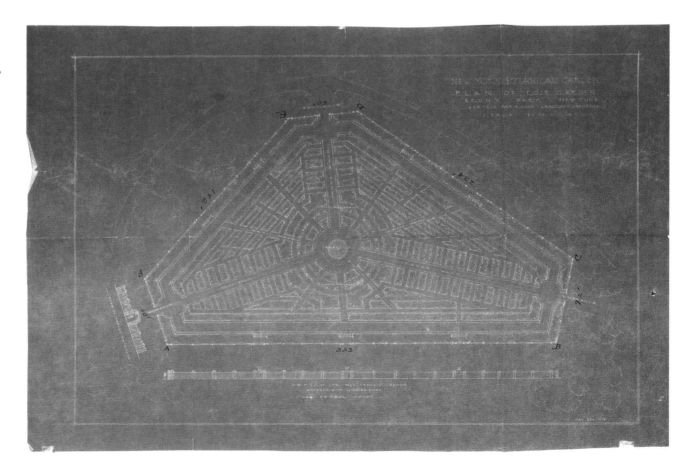

found, where species roses that are parents of the hybrids flower and where the oldest varieties are planted. In the center of the garden, the beds display so-called modern roses, that is, roses developed in the last century and a half with particular horticultural characteristics, including the familiar hybrid tea roses and culminating in the most recent varieties known as landscape roses—shrub roses that flower repeatedly and resist the pests and diseases that can afflict many hybrid teas.

This garden was not completed at the time it was originally designed. The stone entrance steps were built and many roses were planted, but the full design was not completed until 1988. At that time, a generous gift from David Rockefeller in honor of his wife, Peggy, made it possible to complete Farrand's vision for a Rose Garden at the New York Botanical Garden.

OPPOSITE
The Beatrix Jones Farrand plan is seen clearly from the grass terrace above the stairs.

LEFT
The central stone path and the rose-covered gazebo provide a strong focal point in a fragrant sea of flowers.

Today the Rose Garden displays more than three thousand roses representing all the types of roses grown throughout history. Climbing roses blanket the lattice boundary fence and the central gazebo. Hybrid teas, floribundas, grandifloras, musk, noisette, and new shrub roses are displayed in the central beds—including the annual All-American Rose Selections winners. The Rose Garden plantings showcase new and promising rose varieties for gardeners in the northeast. Each year new commercially available varieties are added, and all of the roses are evaluated for flower, fragrance, foliage, disease and insect resistance, and vigor. The roses are labeled, and results of the evaluation are published and distributed at the Garden so that gardeners can look for the best varieties to grow at home.

OPPOSITE AND ABOVE
The Rose Garden exhibits hybrid tea, hybrid perpetual, floribunda, climbing, rambling, old shrub, and new shrub roses. June and September are the best months.

The Rose Garden has two peak flowering seasons, the first in June and then an unexpected "rose encore" in September. Perhaps it is the slanting light, the early evenings, or the knowledge that the season has turned to autumn, but to see the Rose Garden in nearly full flower while the autumn light plays on the lovely colors of the flowers and their fragrance lifts on the cool evening air is a paradisiacal experience indeed.

RIGHT

A rose is not a rose is not a rose, as Garden visitors learn by observing the multiplicity of form, color, and scent to be found in this magnificent Rose Garden. The rose in the upper left corner on this page is the Peggy Rockefeller rose, named in honor of a longtime member of the governing board of the Botanical Garden for whom the Rose Garden itself is named.

OPPOSITE

The Rose Garden is luxuriant in spring and fall and very beautiful even in the hot summer months.

This beautiful Eglantine rose, grown in the garden of Empress Joséphine at Malmaison and illustrated there by the great French botanical illustrator Pierre-Joseph Redouté, is similar to roses being grown today in the Peggy Rockefeller Rose Garden.

Roses grown as standards in containers vary the visual texture.

Rosa Eglanteria var. punicea.

Rosier Eglantier var. couleur ponceau.

P.J. Redouté pinx.

Imprimerie de Rimond

Coutan sculp.

PEONY COLLECTION

Peonies are among the world's most treasured garden plants, both herbaceous peonies, which die to the ground each year, and so-called tree peonies. The herbaceous peony, whose large, waterlily-like flowers are part of many May gardens, is the more familiar garden plant. In contrast, tree peonies are hardy deciduous shrubs, whose stems remain above ground and grow each year, as do other woody shrubs.

The Garden's herbaceous peonies, including forty named varieties, are grown in a striking border that extends for the length of Perennial Garden Way along the edge of the conifer arboretum near the Conservatory. Tree peonies are set in a handsome geometric arrangement of beds above and overlooking the Rose Garden. The collection comprises more than two hundred primarily Chinese tree peony selections, accompanied by selected Japanese and American varieties. They flower in May, when the full, saucer-sized flowers are a fragile and rare pleasure.

OPPOSITE
Herbaceous peonies line Perennial Garden Way in front of the Conservatory.

ABOVE
A living encyclopedia of new and old varieties of herbaceous peonies extends in a border hundreds of feet long, making peony selection for the home gardener a sensual pleasure.

A WORLD OF PLANTS

Not far north of the concrete and steel of Manhattan, there is a living, growing tropical rain forest, a dry cactus-filled desert, a cool and misty cloud forest, and a mercurial landscape that changes from a Renaissance garden to a Japanese autumn garden to a woodland glade full of spring flowers to a village animated by garden-scale trains, and into yet other gardens with each change of the seasons. All of these plant worlds are found within one structure: the Enid A. Haupt Conservatory.

The Conservatory is a grand Victorian-style crystal palace made up of eleven interconnected glasshouse galleries, which are arranged in a symmetrical, rectilinear "C" shape around two elegant pools. The centerpiece is a magnificent glass dome that features the largest collection of New World palms under glass. The other ten glasshouse galleries are arranged in pairs on either side of the Palm Dome, each one displaying a different natural habitat and offering visitors an environmental tour around the world.

These displays of plant life are set inside one of the most extraordinary historic glass structures in the world. In the early days of the Garden, at the end of the nineteenth century, the founders were inspired to re-create in America the experience of the great glasshouses of the Royal Botanic Gardens, Kew. The first director of the New York Botanical Garden, Nathaniel Lord Britton, and his wife, Elizabeth, who were enthralled with the glass Palm House at Kew, were successful in garnering enough financial support to build such an architectural gem in New York. The preeminent American glasshouse firm of the time, Lord & Burnham, was hired to design the Garden's own crystal palace. Although Lord & Burnham designed a number of important conservatories during the late nineteenth and early twentieth century, none can compare with their glasshouse for the New York Botanical Garden.

At the time of the Conservatory's completion in 1902, the exotic plants were displayed in a style popular during that era. That is, the individual specimen plants were each grown in pots that were arranged throughout the glass galleries according to botanical relationships, so that closely related plants were displayed next to each other, regardless of their provenance, habitat, or place of origin. The Victorians were excited to view the myriad curiosities of exotic plants and to understand their relationship to each other in a systematic way; they were less concerned with how the plants fit into a larger ecosystem or habitat biology; indeed, the field of ecology did not formally exist at that time. All of the tropical and subtropical plant collections were rare treasures from far-flung parts of the globe.

PREVIOUS SPREAD
Japanese maples and chrysanthemums are featured in the annual Japanese garden exhibition organized by Garden horticulturists in one of the courtyards of the Conservatory.

RIGHT
The Conservatory's immense reflecting pools provide a mirrored background for the world's most beautiful aquatic plants.

OPPOSITE
The Palm Dome reflects the sunset on a gorgeous October day in New York City.

More than one hundred years later, the Conservatory still contains rare treasures, but the shape of the collections has changed dramatically. As part of the significant restoration in 1997, an examination of the plant collections and how they were displayed led to new and exciting ideas about how the mysterious and dramatic world of tropical and subtropical plants could be better brought to life for the education and enjoyment of visitors. The work of exhibition designer Jon Coe, along with Garden staff and other consultants, led to a new approach in the exhibition of the plants. Today all Conservatory horticulture, often recognized as the world's most beautiful, is under the direction of Francisca Coehlo, Director of Glasshouses.

One of the cruciform galleries of the Conservatory sits regally on well-kept turf.

In this wide view of the west façade of the Conservatory, one can see important European sculpture by Lachaise, Rodin, Marini, and Duchamp-Villon, all part of a major exhibition drawn from the collections of the Museum of Modern Art. The modernist garden setting created in the courtyards to display the sculpture was designed by Susan Cohen.

The Conservatory's eleven glasshouse galleries are now designed to offer an in-depth experience of a series of tropical plant habitats and living collections. Diverse natural habitats of tropical rain forests and American and African deserts complement collections of tropical palms, aquatic and climbing plants, and special collections of carnivorous plants and hanging baskets. Two galleries are devoted to changing seasonal exhibitions of horticultural interest. All exhibitions are interpreted with simple informative signs, audio guides, and publications. This delightful array of educational and ever-changing exhibitions offers visitors, teachers, school groups, specialists, artists, gardeners, and researchers a rich experience of the tropical plant world on every visit to the Conservatory.

PALMS OF THE AMERICAS

One first enters the Conservatory through the Palms of the Americas Gallery—a grand rotunda one hundred feet across and rising to ninety feet into the double-domed cupola centered over the reflecting pool. The still, dark pool serves as a mirror for the tall palms, cycads, ferns, and orchids that surround it. In the Palm Gallery, the stories of one of the world's most useful groups of plants are told. Palms are used for food, textiles, medicines, and building materials for the tropical peoples of the world.

Members of the plant family Arecaceae, palms are mostly found growing in the warm, moist tropics. The more than 2,500 species of palms include some of the most beautiful tropical trees known to humanity. Walking through the collection in the Palm Gallery, one encounters great

OPPOSITE

The Conservatory was originally constructed of limestone, cast iron, steel, and bald-cypress. During its comprehensive restoration in the 1990s, however, bald-cypress, an increasingly rare native species, was not used.

LEFT

In this 1942 photograph, Garden arborists are seen moving an immense palm. In the early twenty-first century, Garden horticulturists are still widely respected for their ability to ball and burlap huge trees in this traditional manner.

specimen palm trees, including the royal palm (*Roystonea regia*), with its smooth, striped trunk, and the coconut palm (*Cocos nucifera*). Thanks to the ability of the coconut fruit to float long distances over water and to germinate and grow upon landing, the coconut palm has colonized the maritime tropics so prolifically that researchers are still working to determine its original habitat. The coconut has been important to humanity worldwide for centuries; coconut milk is one of the most nutritious substances available in nature.

The cycads form another important collection in the Palm Gallery. These primitive relatives of more familiar gymnosperms, such as pines and spruces, are survivors of prehistoric times—their origins date back more than 230 million years. Some cycads, including the large, dramatic queen sago (*Cycas circinalis*), are exquisitely adapted to demanding environments, a characteristic that has insured their persistence in nature for so many millions of years. The queen sago cycad in the Conservatory is a good example of this survival instinct because it survived the 1997 restoration without being moved. Cycads reproduce with large, fuzzy cones that contain the seed; in some years you can see these cones on cycads in the collection.

Cycads are now the subject of a new arena of research—genomics, or the study of a plant's entire genome. Cycads produce chemicals that are identical to neurochemicals found in people, and Garden scientists are at work on an exciting collaborative project to investigate the genetic control of production of these chemicals, which could have great implications for medical research in humans.

OPPOSITE LEFT

This striking botanical illustration of one of the world's most beautiful palms, *Mauritius,* is from the great historical book about palms, *Historia Naturalis Palmarum,* which is in the Library collections.

OPPOSITE CENTER

The round reflecting pool in the Palm Gallery is not original but was created during the 1994–97 restoration.

OPPOSITE RIGHT

Cycads are exhibited in the Palm Gallery, but they are not related to palms; they are more closely related to ferns.

ABOVE

The dome of the Conservatory, which rises to ninety feet (or about nine stories) above the floor, is made entirely of glass and steel.

LOWLAND TROPICAL RAIN FOREST

Leaving the Palm Gallery, one enters a lowland rain forest, where plant collections are displayed to re-create a typical tropical rain forest habitat at an elevation less than about three thousand feet above sea level. High temperature, humidity, and moderate light are the conditions in which these lowland rain forest plants thrive. The canopy is layered so that the tops of tall trees receive the most light, and that is where you find dramatically beautiful epiphytes—orchids and bromeliads, as well as ferns, and even rare cycads, such as *Zamia pseudoparasitica*.

RIGHT

Palms growing in the Americas have been a subject of study by the Botanical Garden for many generations. This is how a pressed specimen of a palm frond looks when it is prepared for filing in the Herbarium.

OPPOSITE

Heliconias, gingers, and bromeliads grow profusely in the Lowland Tropical Rain Forest Gallery.

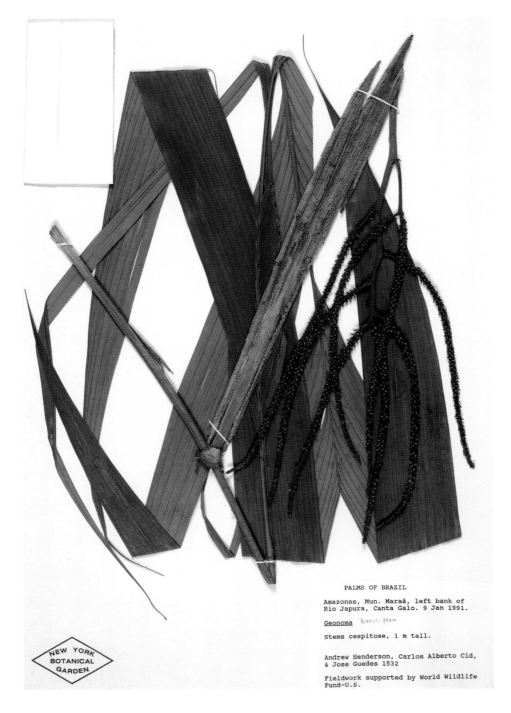

PALMS OF BRAZIL

Amazonas, Mun. Maraã, left bank of
Rio Japura, Canta Galo. 9 Jan 1991.

Geonoma baculifera

Stems cespitose, 1 m tall.

Andrew Henderson, Carlos Alberto Cid,
& Jose Guedes 1532

Fieldwork supported by World Wildlife
Fund-U.S.

NEW YORK
BOTANICAL
GARDEN

Bromeliads every bit as exciting as this one can be seen alive in the rain forest biome exhibitions.

The gallery is arranged for the visitor to walk through the understory and come upon the fallen limb of a tall kapok tree. This huge limb, home to many lowland rain forest epiphytes, provides an opportunity to view plants that spend their entire lives growing in the branches and canopies of tall trees. The fall of a great tree limb such as this creates a light gap in the rain forest canopy. A healer's house, typical of many indigenous dwellings, is displayed here, surrounded by the kinds of plants grown for food and medicine in the lowland rain forest. The well-known anti-cancer plant rosy periwinkle (*Catharanthus roseus*) is just one example. The Healer's House is used for workshops and curatorial demonstrations of how medicines and food are prepared from rain forest plants.

The kapok tree has long been a subject of study at the Botanical Garden, and several examples can be seen in the Conservatory's tropical displays.

The New York Botanical Garden
Ceiba pentandra (L.) Gaertn.
det. P. E. Gibbs, 2001
Boom 8005

The New York Botanical Garden
Plants of Puerto Rico

No. 8005   Bombacaceae

Coco Beach. 18°22'N, 65°46'W. Mangroves and margins. Sea level elev.

Tree. 20 m tall. Flowers pinkish on petals and style, stigma greenish-white, anthers yellow, filaments white.

Brian M. Boom   14 Jan 1988

Assisted by Plant Systematics class, Yale School of Forestry and Environmental Studies. In collaboration with CEER-San Juan.

NEW YORK BOTANICAL GARDEN

Here you will also see the cacao tree (*Theobroma cacao*), the source of chocolate. The large fruits of cacao contain many dark seeds, which are roasted and ground to make cocoa, the raw material from which all chocolate is made. Cacao is pollinated in the wild by nocturnal insects. Here in New York, it is pollinated by hand by the gardeners and by a variety of native insects attracted to the flowers, insuring that there are cacao fruits produced every year. *Theobroma* also demonstrates the phenomenon of cauliflory—that is, the flowers are produced directly from the bark of the tree all along the trunk and branches.

In the next gallery, a skywalk leads up into the taller regions of the lowland rain forest canopy, where one experiences the steady drip of mist that any rain forest explorer would encounter in the wild. These drops are real—a special system in the glasshouse creates the moist droplets that fall gently on both plants and people.

A generation ago, distinguished New York Botanical Garden scientist Bassett Maguire, Ph.D., became the world's expert on the Clusiaceae family of slow-growing tropical evergreens. A beautiful example grows in the Lowland Tropical Rain Forest Gallery.

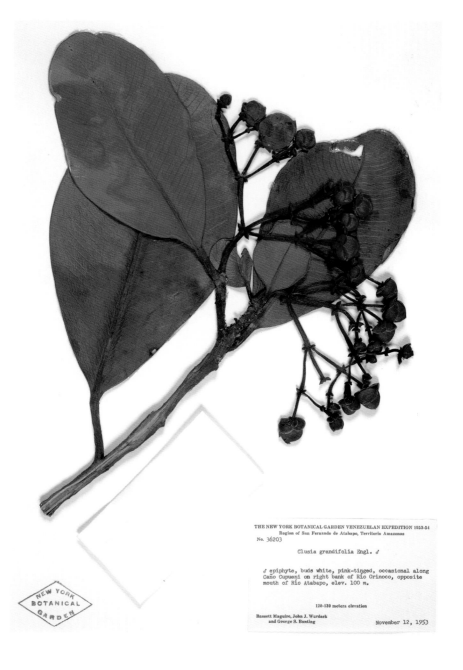

THE NEW YORK BOTANICAL GARDEN VENEZUELAN EXPEDITION 1953-54
Region of San Fernando de Atabapo, Territorio Amazonas
No. 36203

Clusia grandifolia Engl. ♂

♂ epiphyte, buds white, pink-tinged, occasional along
Caño Cupueni on right bank of Río Orinoco, opposite
mouth of Río Atabapo, elev. 100 m.

120-130 meters elevation

Bassett Maguire, John J. Wurdack
and George S. Bunting   November 12, 1953

Many plants on exhibition in the Conservatory are useful ones, bearing fruits, nuts, and other food products. Papaya trees grow and fruit in this exhibition during the New York winter months.

AQUATIC PLANTS AND VINES

In the aquatic plants and vines gallery, lush curtains of tropical vines drape from the arching lattice of the glasshouse roof around an elegant fountain and pool displaying aquatic plants. In the center of the pool is a nineteenth-century French cast-iron fountain surrounded by an array of aquatic plants. These plants, adapted to life in the water, may have special waxy surfaces to keep from becoming waterlogged and specialized tissues to help transport oxygen or float their leaves. The Conservatory's aquatic collection includes the graceful *Cyperus papyrus*, the plant used to make some of the earliest paper.

Known as the jade vine, this plant with a waxy blue-green flower is a showy inhabitant of the Aquatic Plants and Vines Gallery.

A cast-iron fountain is the center-piece of the Aquatic Plants and Vines Gallery, a calm Victorian-style retreat from the drama of the lifelike rain forest biomes.

UPLAND TROPICAL RAIN FOREST

In the Upland Tropical Rain Forest Gallery, tree ferns, orchids, mosses, relatives of blueberries, ferns, bamboos, and other high-elevation plants dangle and weave around the rocks and streams one would find in a montane cloud forest—including a tree fern collected in Mexico by one of the Garden's scientists. The plants in the upland rain forest can all be found growing at relatively high elevations—above three thousand feet and up to ten thousand feet. This cool, misty habitat is one of the most fragile and unusual tropical biomes in the world, where some of the rarest plants may be found.

Many bromeliads can also be found here. An example is *Alcantarea imperialis*, one of the world's largest terrestrial bromeliads. The huge, silvery leaves (as long as two to three feet) are borne in a whorl around the central growing point. This plant lives perched on rocky slopes and has evolved a special adaptation for gathering water and nutrients from this difficult location. Water pools and collects in the plant's crown at the bases of its waxy leaves. The specially adapted cells in the leaf base tissue allow the leaves to absorb water and dissolved nutrients directly—a function reserved for roots in most plants.

OPPOSITE
In the montane rain forests of the world, tree ferns provide a majestic canopy for their lower-growing companions.

RIGHT
The giant leaves and pink and white flowers of *Cavendishia grandiflora*, a rare member of the tropical blueberry family

Because the cool, moist Upland Tropical Rain Forest Gallery is home to a remarkable variety of orchids adapted to this habitat, a changing selection of rare orchids is permanently displayed in a special case—a tiny sample of the Garden's collection of more than eight thousand orchids. Orchids form a vast group of plants living in almost every habitat in the world with an estimated thirty thousand species worldwide.

The gallery is also home to a rich collection of ferns and mosses. Ferns are among the oldest living types of plants on Earth, and their graceful beauty is distinctive in both temperate and tropical regions. One of the most dramatic of the ferns is a great tree fern, *Sphaeropteris horrida*. This species is native to the cool, moist mountains of Mexico and was grown from spores collected by a Garden scientist working in the wild.

Another group of plants native to the upland rain forest are the wild blueberry relatives found growing in the New World cloud forests. These plants are members of the same botanical family, Ericaceae, as cranberries, azaleas, and rhododendrons, and they are very closely related to blueberries. In fact, their waxy flowers, often in shades of bright pink and white, or scarlet and salmon, mature into fruits that look like blueberries. This group of plants is highly endangered in the wild, and Garden horticulturists work with Garden botanists to study, propagate, preserve, and return plants to their native ranges.

RIGHT
Garden scientist James Luteyn, Ph.D., collects tropical blueberries such as the one in this pressed specimen from Central America. Living specimens of these rarely cultivated epiphytes can be seen in the Upland Tropical Rain Forest Gallery.

FAR RIGHT
The rich colors of the flowers of the tropical blueberry family are perfectly rendered in this plate.

The Upland Tropical Rain Forest Gallery displays diverse plants that thrive in cool, moist conditions.

DESERTS OF THE AMERICAS AND AFRICA

The Conservatory displays both American and African desert habitats and plants. Dramatically different from the lush rain forests, deserts are habitats with very scarce rainfall and little available water. The plants that grow in these areas have adapted to this dry and challenging climate by developing, for example, thick skin, special water-storage tissues, minimal leaves, or other surfaces from which water can evaporate, and heavily waxed leaves and trunks to further retard water loss.

In the Deserts of the Americas Gallery, a stark, sandy plain is peppered with bizarre cacti and other desert plants native to American deserts. This landscape has a surreal aspect, with huge-leaved blue agaves keeping company with shining, golden barrel cacti, and includes an incredibly

rare double-trunked boojum tree from Baja California (*Fouquieria columnaris*). The many species of cacti flower from spring to early summer, and their bright floral colors contrast with the grays and silver of the desert foliage. Across from the boojum tree, the skeleton of an American desert icon stands against the curving glass of the gallery: the saguaro cactus (*Carnegiea gigantea*) with its familiar upstretched "arms," a slow-growing native of the Sonoran desert. The live saguaros in the Conservatory have a single trunk because they are young, nursery-grown plants—much younger than the venerable giants of the desert, which have side branches and can be hundreds of years old.

The Deserts of Africa Gallery showcases the cactus look-alikes, the euphorbias. These two very different plant families, native to continents across the ocean from each other, have evolved very similar morphological adaptations to their dry desert homes, a process called convergent

New World desert plants revel in the hot and dry conditions provided for them inside the Conservatory.

evolution. Among the other plants grown here are the "living stones," or *Lithops,* and their close allies, which grow in rocky desert environments, where most of the body of each plant stays underground. The tissue that appears above the surface looks like a pair of twin spotted stones lying on the rocky ground—excellent camouflage for deflecting predators and a very effective way to minimize water loss. This gallery displays a selection of aloes and their relatives, which are well known for the curative properties of the juices in their waxy leaves, especially for healing burns. But aloes also have beautiful flowers. In late winter each year, African deserts are ablaze with the orange, yellow, crimson, and gold candelabra of aloe flowers, a wonderful escape during the cold gray winters of northeastern North America.

ABOVE LEFT
The deserts of Africa are represented by magnificent specimens of aloes and euphorbias.

ABOVE RIGHT
Native only to the New World, cacti, such as this prickly-pear, often produce spectacular flowers.

OPPOSITE
The spines of desert plants are actually reduced leaves, one of many adaptations these plants have made to dry, harsh habitats, providing excellent protection from hungry and thirsty desert animals.

SPECIAL COLLECTIONS

In the special collections gallery, a wide diversity of plants is shown in hanging containers. Primitive lycopods and ferns dangle overhead, and carnivorous plants are shown in both a case and hanging pots. In the case are carnivorous plants native to wet bogs, where the low-nitrogen environment led these plants to adopt a carnivorous lifestyle to supplement this essential nutrient. Carnivorous plants are not active hunters but have evolved special adaptations to attract insects, hold them fast, and digest their proteins. Venus' flytraps, for example, ensnare and digest insects that land on paired leaf tips, which snap shut in response to motion. Pitcher plants have evolved water-collecting tubular leaves that are lined with downward-facing hairs. When an insect lands on a "pitcher," it can easily fall down into the water but has a very difficult time crawling up and out. As a result, insects are trapped in the pooled water at the bottom of the pitcher, where they slowly dissolve, releasing nutrients that can be absorbed by the leaves. American native pitcher plants, such as *Sarracenia venosa*, are not only fascinating but also beautiful in flower, when they produce yellow or red parasols tilted above the deeply cupped leaves that trap the insects.

In another part of the Conservatory, giant baskets of staghorn ferns and begonias swing like verdant chandeliers overhead.

SEASONAL EXHIBITIONS

The two seasonal exhibition galleries are home to changing thematic gardens in spring, summer, fall, and winter, each on display for several weeks at a time. The shows feature hundreds of exceptional plants of great beauty and horticultural use within a historic, romantic, or creative garden design. These displays offer visitors the chance to experience the character and elements of the gardens of history and the world without leaving their own time zone or city. Recent seasonal exhibitions have included the "Chinese Garden and Peony Show," "New Renaissance Garden," "Victorian Ornamentals," and, during the winter holiday season, the "Holiday Train Show."

The hundreds of plants grown and planted for each seasonal exhibition are replaced as each new show is installed. Almost all of these plants are grown by the staff of the Nolen Greenhouses for Living Collections. These greenhouses, the Garden's propagation range, are behind-the-scenes working glasshouses that support all the horticulture and collections of the Garden, including those of the Conservatory.

LEFT
The azure reflecting pools of the Conservatory provide an elegant foil for traditional Japanese garden structures and Japanese maples in the fall exhibit of bonsai, maples, and chrysanthemums.

ABOVE
A watercolor illustrating a Japanese chrysanthemum in a nineteenth-century Japanese grower's catalogue in the collection of the LuEsther T. Mertz Library

FALL SHOW

Each autumn, a Japanese garden is quietly and elegantly laid into the Conservatory's courtyard. For centuries the seasonal changes of the natural world have been celebrated and revered in Japan, where *Momijigari* is the traditional pastime of taking excursions to view the wonderful palette of changing colors in the fall. At the Garden, Japanese maples (*momiji* in Japanese) are joined by selected bonsai and by trained *kiku*, chrysanthemums grown and pruned into the dramatic shapes and presentations of a centuries-old horticultural art. Japanese garden plants such as bamboo, *Cryptomeria*, pines, Hakone grass, and Japanese ferns enrich the autumn plant palette.

A graceful maple and a hedge of *Cryptomeria* add a Japanese flavor to the Conservatory courtyards.

In October, when the waterlilies that normally enliven the courtyard pools fade, Japanese chrysanthemums take over.

HOLIDAY TRAIN SHOW

The Garden's "Holiday Train Show" has become a beloved tradition in New York City. Each year the Conservatory's seasonal exhibition galleries are transformed into a magical world of historic New York landmarks, all meticulously handcrafted from delicate and intricate natural materials found in the plant kingdom. Throughout this enchanted landscape, garden-scale trains travel on track woven alongside the buildings, across bridges high overhead, and over and around waterfalls and pools.

The trains bustle past models replicating buildings from New York City and the Hudson Valley region and include Garden landmarks, such as the Snuff Mill and the Conservatory. Fashioned from bark, twigs, stems, fruits, seeds, and grasses, they are scaled to their actual counterparts with structural and decorative elements all in place. With windows made of resin and buildings lit from within, the show casts a romantic glow of

The Statue of Liberty, which is made entirely of bark, seeds, straw, and other plant parts, wears a gown fashioned from palm fronds for the Botanical Garden's annual "Holiday Train Show."

The Brooklyn Bridge, constructed of bark and twigs, is twenty feet high and extends forty feet across a walkway in the holiday exhibition.

old New York at twilight during the holiday season. Scenic Fifth Avenue is represented in the city's skyline, which stars the Empire State Building and Chrysler Building. Rockefeller Center includes the Channel Gardens and a miniature live tree. Museums and other cultural institutions are also featured. The Metropolitan Museum of Art, the Solomon R. Guggenheim Museum, and the Frick Collection sit grandly among companion brownstones. The New York Public Library resides elegantly within the display—complete in every detail, including the famous twin lions that flank the library's grand entrance stairway. Among the most popular replicas are the original Yankee Stadium, Grand Central Terminal, the Flatiron Building, and Sunnyside, the historic home of Washington Irving.

Set within the curving, elegant glasshouse galleries and lit by the winter sky, the evocative placement of dwarf conifers and hollies, winter-flowering cyclamen, Christmas cactus, African violets, and other charming diminutive flowers adds to the enchantment of this unique Garden show.

ABOVE LEFT
St. Patrick's Cathedral, fashioned of seeds, acorns, reeds, twigs, and bark, is surrounded by miniature ivies and cyclamen.

ABOVE RIGHT
Washington Irving's picturesque cottage, Sunnyside, nestles in among the Conservatory's camellia collection.

OPPOSITE
The domed Palm Gallery is a perfect setting for holiday festivities.

ORCHID SHOW

The annual "Orchid Show" offers a rare opportunity to step into a bewitching tropical world of irresistible allure. Each year in late winter, the Garden arranges thousands of orchid plants covered with hundreds of thousands of orchid flowers in an exhibition that represents all of the Conservatory's rain forest and seasonal exhibition galleries. The result is a paradise dripping with orchids hanging from arching branches and limbs, reaching up from under the rain forest trees, and climbing on the trunks and branches of flowering tropical trees and vines. Orchids are everywhere. The show often highlights a dramatic set piece from one of the regions where orchids are native plants. It may be a fantastical botanist's camp in Brazil, with its walls covered with lianas and rare miniature orchids, or an immense evocation of a Maya ruin, with layers upon layers of orchids and epiphytes clinging to the crumbling edifice.

Indonesian-style boats packed with exotic orchids float on the reflecting pool in the Palms of the Americas Gallery.

The Conservatory's tropical galleries are resplendent with many thousands of flowering orchids during the annual "Orchid Show."

This show combines the dazzle of horticultural display, including varieties and cultivars possessing undeniable glamour, with the substance of learning about orchid species growing in the wild and how to grow them at home. The orchid has been one of the most popular of all cultivated plants since the first tropical specimens were grown in European glasshouses during the Victorian era. Unfortunately, the orchid's popularity may prove to be its downfall in nature. Wild orchids are under severe threat of extinction from habitat destruction and overcollecting. Because the Garden is committed to orchid research and conservation, its scientists study the botany and ecology of orchids; what they discover is useful to conservation work that will ensure the future of these extraordinary plants in nature.

OPPOSITE
Orchids, Spanish-moss, palms, and tree ferns create an intense visual experience for Conservatory visitors.

RIGHT
A palm-thatched hut is home to perfectly grown vanda orchids in full flower.

The slipper orchids *Paphiopedilum*
Lebaudyanum and Magic Lantern

*Phalaenopsis, Dendrobium,
Renanthera,* and *Cymbidium*

W. Fitch, del. et lith.

Vincent Brooks, Day & Son, imp.

Cattleya Dowiana.

Tab. 33.

Fitch, del. et sculp.

Reeve, imp.

Cattleya guttata, var.

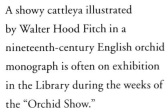

A showy cattleya illustrated
by Walter Hood Fitch in a
nineteenth-century English orchid
monograph is often on exhibition
in the Library during the weeks of
the "Orchid Show."

Another cattleya, illustrated by
Fitch in a famous orchid book
by Sir William Jackson Hooker,
the nineteenth-century English
naturalist

Spring Flower Show

Outside the Conservatory, spring at the Garden is a progressive flower show throughout the landscape, starting with early bulbs and witch-hazels, turning to daffodils and tulips, flowering cherries, magnolias, crabapples, rare alpines in the Rock Garden, perennials of all kinds, lilacs, peonies, and more, eventually culminating in a sea of roses in the Rose Garden.

Inside the Conservatory, spring arrives early with the "Spring Flower Show," an extravaganza including tens of thousands of flowers of all kinds. In the Garden's Nolen Greenhouses for Living Collections, a state-of-the-art production facility that comprises eight growing zones and nearly an acre of growing space, hundreds of different kinds of flowers are brought into flower at the same time. Bulbs are chilled and flowered on a complex schedule so that snowdrops, crocus, tulips, and daffodils may be combined in ways that would be impossible in an outdoor garden. Perennials, shrubs, and even flowering trees are fooled into thinking it is their natural time to flower, so that the horticultural theater of the flower show can include these plants in a spring garden under glass. The plants are beautifully displayed in the seasonal exhibition galleries in settings designed to evoke gardens of different periods and regions.

Themes have included such intriguing examples as the "New Renaissance Garden," an evocation of a Renaissance Revival garden in Italy, with terra-cotta pots full of flowers and bulbs set under an elegant portico and a fountain garden encircled by tall cypresses. "American Woodland Garden" featured a series of beds and borders set in a woodland created with birches, maples, and small flowering trees. The plantings in this special exhibition change regularly throughout the duration of the show.

RIGHT
Unusual combinations are possible in the horticultural theater of flower shows. Here foxgloves poke up through a Japanese maple, but the effect is splendid, and no one seems to mind the peculiar juxtaposition.

FAR RIGHT
The first flush of color in the "Spring Flower Show" is achieved with tulips, daffodils, and other spring bulbs.

Thousands of foxgloves and delphiniums are forced into bloom in the Garden's propagation greenhouses and then moved into the spring show when they are in perfect flower.

SUMMER SHOWS

As in the spring, summer brings a group of special exhibitions to the Conservatory. "Victorian Ornamentals" presents a palette of bright tropical plants laid out in the Victorian bedding tradition of regular geometries with bold textures and colors woven together. A sparkling fountain usually centers the scene, surrounded with such large-leaved plants as *Colocasia, Anthurium,* and *Caladium.* Throughout the long double borders, a wide variety of canna lilies are grown. Cannas such as 'Tropicana', with its multicolored striped leaves and bold, tangerine-sherbet flowers, compete for attention with new coleus varieties. New annuals are grown in containers and mixed together with ferns and other traditional Victorian favorites. Tree ferns, palms, and even bananas add scale to the grand Victorian borders.

Another annual summer feature is "Waterlilies and Lotus." Each year, the two elegant reflecting pools in the Conservatory courtyard gradually become lush kaleidoscopes of exotic summer color, thanks to the emergence of the waterlily and lotus collections that are grown in the pools. In the tropical pool, a central ring of water heated to 85 degrees Fahrenheit is watched with great anticipation for the appearance of the giant Amazon

In the summer, the Conservatory is very warm, but canna, caladium, and coleus feel right at home. The effect may be Victorian, but the plants are mainly modern cultivars.

lily, *Victoria amazonica*. This famous waterlily is native to the Amazon region, where it develops a whorl of single leaves that can each extend as much as ten feet across. The leaves are curled up at the edges, and their lower surfaces are covered with dangerous spines that deter predators. In the center of the whorl, large, creamy-white flowers open at night to attract pollinators, which are captured when the flowers close in the morning. At the Garden, the plants are overwintered in a cozy pool in the growing greenhouses and come out for their summer airing in June each year. There, the leaves grow into dramatic dimensions all summer before returning to their winter home under glass.

There are many species of gorgeous waterlilies, and their flowers range from magenta to pink to white to yellow to lavender and purple. Their companions in the pools are a collection of lotus varieties. The lotus *Nelumbo nucifera* is revered as a sacred flower throughout much of its native range in India and Asia. The bluish, waxy foliage rises up out of the water in late spring, followed by very large, showy, magnolia-like flowers that mature into dry seed pods. After maturity, the dry seeds rattle in the pods. One of the most beautiful of aquatic plants, the lotus is available in a range of cultivars with different color flowers. The Garden's collection displays dozens of forms.

OPPOSITE
A southern magnolia in partial flower rises above tropical lotus and the immense floating leaves of the famous Amazon waterlily, *Victoria amazonica*, named for Queen Victoria.

ABOVE LEFT
The Amazon waterlily prepares to flower inside a ring containing heated water. It is grown outdoors because there is no pool inside the Conservatory large enough to contain its massive leaves and rapid growth.

ABOVE RIGHT
The water of the pools is highly reflective because of a harmless dye that is put in by Garden horticulturists to discourage algae.

BELOW LEFT
The Amazon waterlily flowers only in the late afternoon and evening and is pollinated by a special beetle.

BELOW RIGHT
The colors of tropical waterlilies are particularly vivid.

NOLEN GREENHOUSES FOR LIVING COLLECTIONS

Conservatory exhibitions are made possible by this behind-the-scenes growing facility, which was dedicated in 2005. With over an acre under glass, it is one of the world's highest-tech buildings for maintaining living collections and propagating new plants. More than one hundred thousand plants are tended or grown here annually. The New York Botanical Garden's extensive living collections are housed here in eight specially created growing zones, which are adapted to the differing requirements of desert, tropical, and temperate species. For example, there are dedicated zones for alpine plants, for ferns, and for orchids. One square foot of behind-the-scenes growing space is needed for each square foot of exhibition space in the Enid A. Haupt Conservatory. In addition to plants and collections maintained in the greenhouses for public exhibition, the Garden's scientific research faculty members grow and keep plants here for research purposes. The public may visit the Bourke-Sullivan Display House, part of the greenhouse complex, for a unique opportunity to view a behind-the-scenes growing facility, where two special exhibitions are also featured each year.

The Scottish botanical illustrator Walter Hood Fitch created this masterpiece, a depiction of the Amazon waterlily in flower. These plants are raised in the Nolen Greenhouses and moved outside to the Conservatory pools in the summer.

LEFT
Waterlily pads

BELOW LEFT
A collapsing lotus flower

BELOW CENTER
A tropical waterlily

BELOW RIGHT
A lotus flower about to open

In the early 1890s, when Nathaniel Lord Britton toured the Bronx searching for a perfect site for the New York Botanical Garden's permanent home, he visited three locations in what was then a rural oasis at the edge of the expanding city. As we have seen, the site that stood out had rolling fields punctuated by dark gray rock outcrops and shaded by towering oaks, sweetgums, and tulip trees. It had a sparkling river that rushed through a rocky gorge in the middle of an ancient forest and "deep and loamy" soil, perfect for growing plants from all the corners of the globe. Britton knew he had found the Garden's home.

Although the landscape has changed since Britton's time, the Garden retains its natural beauty, in large part because of the many thousands of important trees growing across its 250 acres. The forest remains intact, though changed, and many of the ancient trees that Britton admired still stand today. For more than a hundred years, Garden scientists and horticulturists have been amassing diverse collections of trees and shrubs from around the world to add to the Garden's rich native flora. These collections serve multiple missions. As research tools, they are important for the study of plant evolution, physiology, and morphology; as reference collections, they are used by professional horticulturists and home gardeners to assess the merits of ornamental plants; and as inspiring elements of a beautiful garden, they provide year-round delight to visitors and define the character of the Garden's landmark landscape.

ARTHUR AND JANET ROSS CONIFER ARBORETUM

The conifers, or cone-bearing plants, stand out among the Garden's tree collections. The oldest intact plant collection is the Arthur and Janet Ross Conifer Arboretum, a collection of mature pines, spruces, and firs planted across nearly forty acres of rolling terrain and rock outcrops between the Conservatory and the Library. From a towering Himalayan pine (*Pinus wallichiana*) near the Leon Levy Visitor Center, to a planting of rare tiger tail spruces (*Picea polita*) near the Garden Cafe, to a grove of Nikko fir (*Abies homolepis*) by the Home Gardening Center, the plantings in the Conifer Arboretum are unequaled anywhere in the world.

PREVIOUS SPREAD

The American tulip tree (*Liriodendron tulipifera*) is native to the Garden's site. An older tree in the area inspired Nathaniel Lord Britton to plant, in 1903, this matched set, arranged in a double allée horseshoe drive leading to the Library.

OPPOSITE

A set of romantic white pines rises above one section of the Perennial Garden.

RIGHT

A botanical illustration of white pine

FAR RIGHT

A herbarium specimen of white pine

Mature pines cover much of the Conifer Arboretum, including a grove of five Tanyosho pines (*Pinus densiflora* 'Umbraculifera') planted in 1908. This grove is one of the world's most distinguished plantings of Japanese red pine, coveted for its brilliant red bark, sinuous trunks, and spreading canopy of pale green needles. Near the Tanyosho pines are two mature specimens of lacebark pine (*P. bungeana*). Planted in 1909, these trees have dark green needles that contrast with dazzling bark that peels from the trunk in an intricate pattern of greens, grays, and white.

ABOVE
One of the Garden's greatest treasures, a grove of mature Tanyosho pines stands near the Leon Levy Visitor Center.

RIGHT
The Tanyosho pine grove in winter

OPPOSITE
At the right in the photo is a specimen of the lacebark pine of China, celebrated for its mottled white bark.

Stately spruces surround the cafe. Mature specimens of Colorado spruce (*Picea pungens*) demonstrate the range of needle color, from powder blue to bright green, found in this species. They contrast in form and foliage with the dark green spires of eighty-year-old specimens of Oriental spruce (*P. orientalis*) and the grayish-blue needles of a young Brewer's weeping spruce (*P. breweriana*), which was planted near the cafe in 2002. The regular addition of new species to the collection will ensure that the Conifer Arboretum can continue to be a vibrant place for the study of conifers into the next century and beyond.

RIGHT

A majestic Himalayan pine in the Leon Levy Visitor Center

FAR RIGHT

A cheerful blue Colorado spruce in the Ross Conifer Arboretum

OPPOSITE

In the Conifer Arboretum, flowering cherries are interplanted with the conifers, which provide a strong, dark background for the pastel cherry flowers.

Of all the majestic conifers, none are more remarkable than the firs. Firs are mountain plants and not considered well suited to urban environments. It is unlikely that the fir collection, which includes Japanese nikko and momi firs (*Abies homolepis* and *A. firma*), Greek and silver firs (*A. cephalonica* and *A. alba*) from Europe, and white fir (*A. concolor*) from the American West, could be re-established in this latitude under current climatic conditions. Garden horticulturists are experimenting with the addition of firs from warm climates, including the Algerian fir (*A. numidica*), in the hope that firs will continue to grace the Conifer Arboretum in spite of the changing climate.

A grove of mature Nikko firs, native to Japan, stands near Perennial Garden Way in the center of the Arthur and Janet Ross Conifer Arboretum.

There is a single specimen of the giant sequoia in the Garden collection, but it will not grow to this great height for many generations.

TULIP TREES

Between 1903 and 1906, twenty-four young tulip trees (*Liriodendron tulipifera*) were planted in two double rows along the drive in front of the then-recently completed Library building. These handsome specimens joined a venerable and massive tulip tree, known as the "mother tree," which was already growing at the site. Workers had carefully protected this awe-inspiring tree during the construction of the building and adjacent roadways.

More than a century later, this parade of tulip trees, now known as the Tulip Tree Allée, has become a beloved symbol of the Garden and one of New York City's most remarkable tree plantings. The mother tree is over one hundred feet tall with a broad, furrowed trunk five feet thick at the base. In spring, the canopies of the tulip trees become bright green as their unmistakable four-lobed leaves gradually unfold. In early summer, green and orange flowers poke through the fully expanded leaves, and in fall, the leaves light up the sky as they turn a brilliant clear yellow. Winter may be the most beautiful season for the tulip trees, as their tall, dark trunks and spreading canopies can be fully appreciated against a carpet of freshly fallen snow.

OPPOSITE

The double allée of tulip trees lends scale as well as glorious color to the view uphill to the Library building.

LEFT

The distinctive leaves of the tulip tree, with four large, pointed lobes, as well as the cupped orange and green flowers, are easy to recognize in the herbarium specimen on the left and in the fine botanical illustration on the right.

In May a spectrum of flowers explodes into bloom beneath the high shade of tulip trees, oaks, maples, and sweetgums along Azalea Way. Members of the rhododendron group, hundreds of azalea and rhododendron species and hybrids are planted across this long wooded slope. Flowering starts in late March, when the lavender flowers of the early flowering Korean rhododendron (*Rhododendron mucronulatum*) open on naked stems, and continues through April and May, when the varied and beautiful flowers of Asian species and hybrid and native azaleas open. The long show of color along Azalea Way ends as late as early July when the last of the Dexter hybrid rhododendrons to flower finally open.

The plantings on Azalea Way were first installed in the 1940s. Early plantings included swamp azalea (*R. viscosum*) and other powerfully fragrant deciduous azaleas from the eastern United States alongside a range of species and hybrid azaleas from Asia, including the delicate pink-flowered princess azalea (*R. schlippenbachii*).

Over the years, the plantings have been expanded. In 1981 hundreds of Japanese azalea species and hybrids donated by the former Eberstadt estate on Long Island were planted next to existing specimens in the collection. Today Azalea Way features a good cross-section of the diverse *Rhododendron* genus. Plans for further development of this area include the creation of an educational display that describes the story of rhododendrons and azaleas both in nature and in gardens.

A species of rhododendron as illustrated in the nineteenth century in *Curtis's Botanical Magazine*

Although this photograph would indicate otherwise, the Garden's azalea and rhododendron collections are in serious need of rejuvenation and enrichment, a project slated for completion within the next few years.

CRABAPPLES

In late April or early May, after the last daffodils on Daffodil Hill have faded, the Garden's extensive Bruckmann crabapple collection (*Malus* species and cultivars) bursts into bloom. Orderly rows of crabapples planted along Daffodil Hill, ranging from rare species such as *M. tschonoskii* to horticultural selections such as the heirloom *M. toringo* 'Fuji' and more recent introductions such as *M.* 'Molten Lava', light up the spring sky with flowers ranging from pure white to deep burgundy. The intensity of this spring bloom is matched in autumn, when the fruits mature. These miniature versions of the domestic apple range from tiny golden globes to cheerful russet apples two inches across.

Crabapples have always been an important part of the Garden's living collections of plants. The first specimens were planted on the grounds in an area near Twin Lakes, and in the late 1930s the collection was moved to its current location in the southwestern corner of the grounds. Here, crabapples are planted along the paths so that visitors can linger among them, comparing flowers and fruit and deciding which of these trees they would most like to have in their own gardens.

ABOVE LEFT AND RIGHT
The crabapple collection now contains many old and new specimens, having been substantially expanded in recent years in memory of Donald J. Bruckmann.

OPPOSITE
These young crabapples are planted at the edge of historic Daffodil Hill.

The diversity and age of the Garden's crabapple collection make it a great resource for professional horticulturists as well. The combination of wild species, heirloom selections, and new introductions allows researchers to compare the disease resistance, as well as the length and intensity of flowering and fruiting of more than ninety different species and cultivars. Such studies inform the nursery industry as to which crabapples perform best in an urban environment and help to make all of our gardens healthier and more beautiful.

RIGHT

With a grove of North American white pines in the distance, daffodils and crabapples present their May show in the foreground.

OPPOSITE

In the Benenson Ornamental Conifers, a portrait of one of the Garden's several mature blue Atlas cedars, which are rarely seen nowadays in their native habitat, the High Atlas Mountains of Morocco

BENENSON ORNAMENTAL CONIFERS

The Benenson Ornamental Conifers grow in a landscape of mature shade trees and stunning rock outcrops between the Bronx River and the Nolen Greenhouses for Living Collections. From century-old blue Atlas cedars (*Cedrus atlantica* 'Glauca') to miniature white pines, the Benenson collection includes dwarf and other unusual conifers of all sizes, shapes, and colors. These combine with the specimens in the Arthur and Janet Ross Conifer Arboretum to make the Garden's conifer collection one of the most diverse and beautiful in the world.

The Benenson conifers incorporate the historic Montgomery conifers donated to the Garden in 1947 and originally displayed in a landscape plan designed by Marian Cruger Coffin that opened to the public in 1949. Coffin drew from her experience working with Henry Francis DuPont at Winterthur in Delaware to create a design that preserved the natural beauty of the site, while highlighting the beauty and diversity of the conifers. Among the dozens of plants that remain from the Montgomery donation is the "type" specimen of the Montgomery blue spruce (*Picea pungens* 'R. H. Montgomery'). Over seventy five-years old, it is a powder-blue pyramid fifteen feet tall and twelve feet wide at the base. All Montgomery spruces in cultivation are descended from this mother plant.

OPPOSITE
The grove of dawn-redwoods, a deciduous conifer, in all its winter glory

ABOVE
Seen from a high rock outcropping, blue-tinged conifers, such as the blue Atlas cedar on the right and the young Arizona cypress in the center foreground, mix colorfully with green conifers against a background of brilliant oaks.

RIGHT
Dwarf conifers of every description nestle among the rocks.

By the year 2000, the original plantings and landscape had deteriorated, so between 2000 and 2004 the Garden staff completely restored the fifteen-acre site and added more than 250 new conifers to the collection. Restoration work was based on a design concept by Patrick Chassé, inspired by Marian Coffin's original plans, which he had discovered in the archives at Winterthur. Landscape architect Shavaun Towers translated Chassé's concept into a detailed restoration plan, which included the construction of never-realized stone-and-cedar pavilions from Coffin's original design and two new dwarf conifer display beds, one in the shade and the other in full sun.

OPPOSITE
A rustic stone and cedar pavilion blends beautifully with diverse plantings in the Benenson Ornamental Conifers.

ABOVE
The conifers are magical after a snowfall.

Today the collection includes more than four hundred dwarf conifers and other unusual varieties. Irreplaceable mature specimens, such as an eerie snakebranch spruce (*Picea abies* 'Virgata'), grow alongside new introductions, including a group of eastern white pine (*Pinus strobus*) cultivars selected by Dr. Sidney Waxman of the University of Connecticut. The new plantings celebrate more than forty years of his work growing, selecting, and introducing conifers for gardens. The ornamental conifer collection features his best introductions, ranging from the adorable miniature white pine *Pinus strobus* 'Sea Urchin', a dense, spiky cushion of blue-green needles, to the chaotic *Larix* 'Varied Directions', a deciduous conifer with branches that spread at all angles from the trunk.

ABOVE
Dr. Sidney Waxman selected 'Sea Urchin' from a crop of eastern white pine seedlings.

RIGHT
A kaleidoscope of slow-growing pines, spruces, and other conifers in the display of dwarf conifers

OPPOSITE
Ornamental conifers grow in every size and shape, from the graceful wave of hemlocks to the precision of dawn-redwoods to the unpredictability of weeping giant sequoias.

The restored Benenson conifers have expanded the opportunities for Garden horticulturists to experiment with new plant material. A grove of five weeping giant sequoias (*Sequoiadendron giganteum* 'Pendulum') planted near the new entrance pavilions is proof that this tender conifer has a chance of surviving the Garden's cold and unpredictable climate. A young monkey puzzle tree (*Araucaria araucana*), native to Chile and Argentina, is tucked in among some of the mature conifers. If it survives, this will be the first conifer from the Southern Hemisphere ever successfully grown outdoors at the Garden.

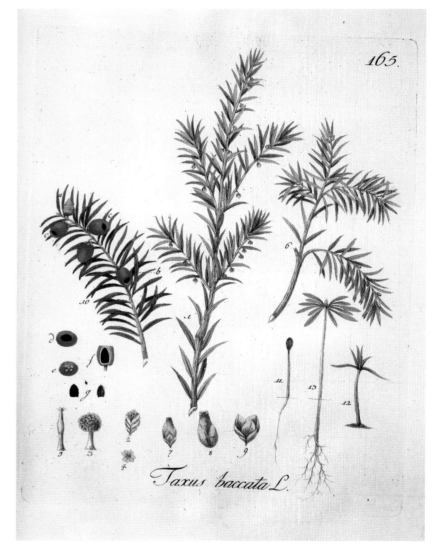

Cedar of Lebanon was beautifully illustrated in *Allgemeines Deutsches Garten-magazin* in the late eighteenth century. Newly planted cedars can now be seen in the Benenson conifers.

An English yew from the pages of Johann Simon Kerner's *Figures des Plantes Economiques*, a multivolume set published from 1786 to 1796.

MAPLES

In the fall, Americans travel to New England and other mountainous or northern regions to revel in the fiery autumn brilliance of maples, just as people from Tokyo journey to the mountains to see Japanese maples at their peak. An October visit to the Garden's maple collection, which is next to the Benenson conifers, combines the pleasures of both of these traditional excursions. The maple collection, established in the 1940s, comprises a wide range of maple species and cultivars, including colorful native species and rare selections from Japan and China.

Dozens of unusual maples can be found in the collection, including a remarkable trident maple (*Acer buergerianum*) from China with glossy three-lobed leaves that turn yellow in fall and bark that peels from the trunk in long, thin strips. A rare devil's maple (*A. diabolicum*) from

A famous specimen of paper-bark maple is shown to great effect against blue spruces.

This coral bark maple is a spectacular plant for the winter garden.

Japan grows nearby at the base of one of the Garden's many exposed outcrops. The chartreuse twigs of a young *A. nipponicum*, also from Japan, are as beautiful in the winter as the thick, feltlike leaves are in the middle of summer.

Although many of the Garden's rarest maples are found in the maple collection, other maples grow elsewhere in the Garden. Red and sugar maples (*Acer rubrum* and *A. saccharum*) brighten the forest in fall, and the sinewy trunks of a weeping Japanese maple seem to grow directly from a rock ledge in front of the Stone Cottage. A handful of Japanese maple cultivars is sprinkled across the slope in front of the entrance to the Rock Garden. The Garden's most beautiful maple is probably a mature paperbark maple (*A. griseum*), which is planted among spruces in the Ross Conifer Arboretum. Its red bark, which peels from the trunk in irregular strips, seems to glow against the blue and green needles of the surrounding spruces.

OPPOSITE
Old sugar maples and oaks line a sinuous path across a well-kept lawn.

LEFT
There is nothing shy about this venerable specimen of Japanese maple in its fall guise.

ABOVE
The intricate leaves in this herbarium specimen are similar to those of several Japanese maple cultivars in the Garden's living collections.

LILACS

Before the roses in the Peggy Rockefeller Rose Garden begin to flower, the southeastern corner of the Garden comes alive with lilacs. The Garden's extensive lilac collection is planted along a curving slope north of the rose garden. It was established in the late 1940s when approximately five hundred plants from the breeding collection of legendary lilac grower T. A. Havemeyer were planted at the Garden. The original planting was designed by Marian Cruger Coffin, who separated the lilacs with grassy paths so that visitors can get up close to enjoy their powerful fragrance.

The first lilacs to flower are the hyacinthifloras, which begin opening as early as mid-April. One of the most beautiful is *Syringa* × *hyacinthiflora* 'Catinat', with pleasantly fragrant, delicate pink florets. The hyacinthifloras are followed by the French hybrid lilacs, the collective name for cultivars and hybrids of *Syringa vulgaris* from eastern Europe. Many of the most popular and intensely fragrant lilacs are in this group, including the double-flowered purple 'Adelaide Dunbar' and the beautiful white 'Miss Ellen Willmott'. The last lilacs to flower are the tree lilacs, *S. pekinensis* and *S. reticulata*, whose dense clusters of creamy-white flowers may last well into June.

The lilac collection will be expanded as new insect- and disease-resistant selections become available. These plants will be incorporated into the existing collection where Garden visitors can enjoy them at close range.

Cutleaf lilac is cherished for its foliage as well as its flowers.

'Nadezhda' is a wonderfully fragrant and floriferous lilac from Russia.

Pierre-Joseph Redouté illustrated a delicate pink-flowered lilac in Empress Joséphine's garden at Malmaison.

CHERRIES

From the carmine buds of Okame cherry (*Prunus* 'Okame') in late March to the brilliant white petals of mature Sato Zakura cherries (*P. serrulata* cultivars) in early May, the month-long bloom of the Garden's ethereal flowering cherries is proof that spring is here. More than two hundred flowering cherries are planted throughout the Garden's landscape, with the largest and most diverse planting found along a curving path in Cherry Valley, just north of the lilacs. This combines cultivars of early flowering Higan (*P. × subhirtella*) and Yoshino cherries (*P. × yedoensis*), and later-flowering Sato Zakura cherries, including the unusual *P.* 'Ukon' with greenish-white flowers in May.

A flowering cherry, pale blue
sky, very green turf—
a familiar Botanical Garden
sight in spring

Probably New York City's most
revered Japanese flowering
cherry, this 'Akebono' reaches
out elegantly toward the reflecting pool of the Leon Levy
Visitor Center.

One of the weeping cherries
in autumn

A splendid set of Japanese
weeping cherries, given to the
Garden by distinguished
American horticulturist Beth
Straus, lines the spring approach
to the classical Conservatory.

Flowering cherries also grow amid and around the pines, spruces, and firs of the Conifer Arboretum. Spectacular mature specimens, like a massive Edo-Higan cherry (*Prunus pendula* var. *ascendens*) at the entrance to the Rock Garden and an ancient daybreak flowering cherry (*P.* × *yedoensis* 'Akebono') at the Visitor Center have graced the center of the Garden for decades. They are awe-inspiring when they are in flower and again in fall when their leaves become a kaleidoscope of yellow, orange, and burgundy. More recently planted cherries also add drama. The sinuous weeping cherries (*P. pendula*) on the Conservatory terrace are stunning in April, when their pink buds and white flowers are reflected against the curved glass of the Conservatory.

RIGHT

At the entrance to the historic Rock Garden, this flowering cherry is one of the wonders of New York City.

OPPOSITE

The collection contains many hybrids of the Yoshino cherry.

MAGNOLIAS

As winter grinds on through February, the Garden's magnolias begin to stir. During warm spells in late winter, the fuzzy buds of the saucer magnolias (*Magnolia × soulangeana* cultivars) and star magnolias (*M. stellata*) in the magnolia collection and a mature Kobus magnolia (*M. kobus*) on Perennial Garden Way start to swell. When March comes in like a lamb, these magnolias burst into bloom, their flowers an early sign that spring is here, and Garden visitors make annual pilgrimages to see the magnolias in flower. The collection features mature early flowering Asian magnolia species and hybrids such as the pure white-flowered willow-leafed magnolia (*M. salicifolia*) and a variety of saucer magnolias, including a trio of *M. × soulangeana* 'Alexandrina' planted in 1916. Later-flowering American magnolias, such as the sweetly scented sweetbay (*M. virginiana*) and the umbrella magnolia (*M. tripetala*), whose leaves are large enough to keep the rain away, are also planted here.

OPPOSITE
Magnolias are the first trees to flower in the spring.

LEFT
The magnolia collection, concentrated in the grove of new and old specimens, is arranged in a picturesque design.

ABOVE
Magnolia 'Leonard Messel' produces magnificent spring flowers.

Magnolias can also be found elsewhere in the Garden. Southern magnolias (*Magnolia grandiflora*) grace the Ladies' Border and the Conservatory courtyard, their thick, evergreen leaves creating an elegant canvas for the huge, fragrant flowers, which unfold in early summer. Also in the Ladies' Border is a selection of Oyama magnolias (*M. sieboldii*), whose nodding, cup-shape white flowers encircle striking red stamens. A specimen of *M.* 'Elizabeth' grows across from the Perennial Garden not far from the Ladies' Border. This cultivar is one of the many newly introduced yellow-flowered hybrids of our native cucumber magnolia (*M. acuminata*) and Asian species.

OPPOSITE
The southern magnolia, *Magnolia grandiflora*, is seen here in a hand-colored engraving from Mark Catesby's important work *Hortus Europae Americanus*.

LEFT
Magnolias are found not only in the living collections of the Garden, but also in herbarium specimens used by plant scientists.

FOLLOWING SPREAD
Older magnolia trees have a gnarled and romantic habit accentuated by years of careful pruning.

OAKS

One of the marvels of the New York Botanical Garden is an enormous, 245-year-old red oak (*Quercus rubra*) growing along the main trail near the Bronx River, one of dozens of ancient native oaks growing here. Two craggy white oaks (*Q. alba*) that shade the meadow between the Nolen Greenhouses and the Benenson conifers are more than two hundred years old. A black oak of similar vintage is a focal point in the Rock Garden.

Joining these native oaks are hundreds of specimens that have been planted over the last century. One of the most notable is a mature Daimyo oak (*Q. dentata*) by the Mosholu Gate. This rare Japanese species has huge leaves, and thick, feltlike twigs. Together the native and planted oaks lend a sense of permanence and strength to the Garden's landscape.

ABOVE LEFT AND CENTER
Pierre-Joseph Redouté's bold plates for a book by François Michaux illustrate white oak (left) and red oak (center).

ABOVE RIGHT
A herbarium specimen with the leaves and acorns of an English oak. The envelope attached to the herbarium sheet contains pieces of leaf or acorn that have fallen from the specimen.

WITCH-HAZELS

Witch-hazels are unique among the Garden's trees and shrubs. What other plants can be found flowering in December or January when the rest of the Garden is in its deep winter slumber? What other shrubs live for a hundred years, needing only the occasional pruning to restore their youthful vigor? Of the Garden's interesting and beautiful specimens, the grandest is an ancient Chinese witch-hazel (*Hamamelis mollis*), which grows along Conservatory Drive near the Home Gardening Center. Year in and year out, this huge shrub puts on a display of fragrant yellow flowers starting in December. These four-petaled flowers unfurl on days when the temperature remains somewhat warm and then curl back up during cold snaps.

The oldest and most magnificent of the Garden's winter-flowering witch-hazels

Other witch-hazels in the Garden include the native species, *H. virginiana*, which is famous as the source of the soothing astringent; it grows wild in the forest and blooms in late fall. Selections of *H. × intermedia*, a hybrid of Chinese and Japanese (*H. japonica*) witch-hazels, join both its parents and the Ozark witch-hazel (*H. vernalis*) in bloom in a variety of locations throughout the Garden in January and February. A number of outstanding horticultural selections of witch-hazel, including the bright yellow 'Arnold's Promise', the burgundy-flowered 'Diane', and the coppery 'Jelena', can be found in the Perennial Garden and Ladies' Border.

OTHER TREES AND SHRUBS

Since 1895 Garden scientists and horticulturists have added trees and shrubs from around the world to the native trees already in the landscape to create a diverse and beautiful arboretum. Initially, these collections were arranged systematically across the landscape based on theories of plant evolution described in German botanists Adolf Engler and Karl Prantl's nineteenth-century work *Die Natürlichen Pflanzenfamilien* (The Natural

Flowering shrubs add a layer of color to the landscape throughout the year. On the left, a mature hydrangea in the fall; in the center, the same shrub in the summer; on the right, a *Corylopsis* or winter-hazel

Plant Families). In this sequence, closely related trees and shrubs were planted together for ease of comparison and study. The systematic plantings included the Fruticetum (a collection of shrubs), the Viticetum (a collection of vines), and the Deciduous Arboretum (a collection of all hardy trees except conifers), representing all together a wide array of the world's woody plants.

Over time, these original collections have matured and changed. Some of the systematic plantings, including the separate shrub collection, were lost in 1937 when the Garden was reduced in size. Today the Garden's shrubs are integrated into the various display gardens and the larger landscape. Perhaps the most beautiful shrub at the Garden, a mature white enkianthus (*Enkianthus perulatus*), is a highlight in the Rock Garden when its bell-shaped flowers open in May and again when its leaves turn scarlet in October. In addition to the distinguished shrubs in the Rock Garden and other display gardens, collections of hydrangeas, viburnums, and other horticulturally important shrubs can be found in various locations throughout the Garden.

The collections also include a wide range of the world's hardy trees. Some, such as the igiri tree (*Idesia polycarpa*) on the main lawn, which produces long, dangling clusters of red fruits in fall, and a dove tree (*Davidia involucrata*) near the Mosholu Gate, whose flowers are surrounded by large white bracts reminiscent of a dove's wings, are rare in cultivation. Others, such

The collections include several large London plane trees notable for their exfoliating white bark.

as the mammoth London plane (*Platanus × acerifolia*) by the Mosholu Gate and a towering pignut hickory (*Carya glabra*) near the Rock Garden, are more common but irreplaceable because of their great age and size.

The disruption of the original systematic planting sequence has freed Garden horticulturists to plant new trees and shrubs wherever growing conditions are best and where they will have the greatest aesthetic impact. This has created some dazzling combinations in the landscape. A grove of Japanese stewartia (*Stewartia pseudocamellia*), with jigsaw-puzzle bark and white flowers, joins white-barked birches from Europe, Asia, and

ABOVE LEFT
A native pignut hickory in glorious fall color stands sentinel outside the Rock Garden.

ABOVE RIGHT
The highly colored mottled bark of the stewartia makes it as interesting in winter as its fragrant white flowers make it in summer.

OPPOSITE
The brilliant fall foliage of sweet gums is one of the Garden's true delights.

North America to create a contrast with the pines in the Conifer Arboretum. Dogwoods (*Cornus*) and redbuds (*Cercis canadensis*) light up the understory along Azalea Way and thrive in the high shade of the surrounding trees. In May the feathery flowers of a Chinese fringe tree (*Chionanthus retusus*) poke between the canopies of oaks near the Garden Cafe.

Today the Garden's diverse collections of trees and shrubs are resources for botanists and horticulturists, as well as awe-inspiring presences that lend a sense of serenity and permanence to the landscape.

ABOVE LEFT
A topiaried rank of European hornbeams marches alongside the Herbarium building.

ABOVE CENTER
Mature kousa dogwoods rise above the Peggy Rockefeller Rose Garden.

ABOVE RIGHT
Another European hornbeam, this one older and larger, is used as a specimen tree on the lawn near the Library building.

OPPOSITE
The orange and green flowers of the tulip tree are held above its leaves in spring, and although not easy to see, they create a colorful aura in the morning sunlight.

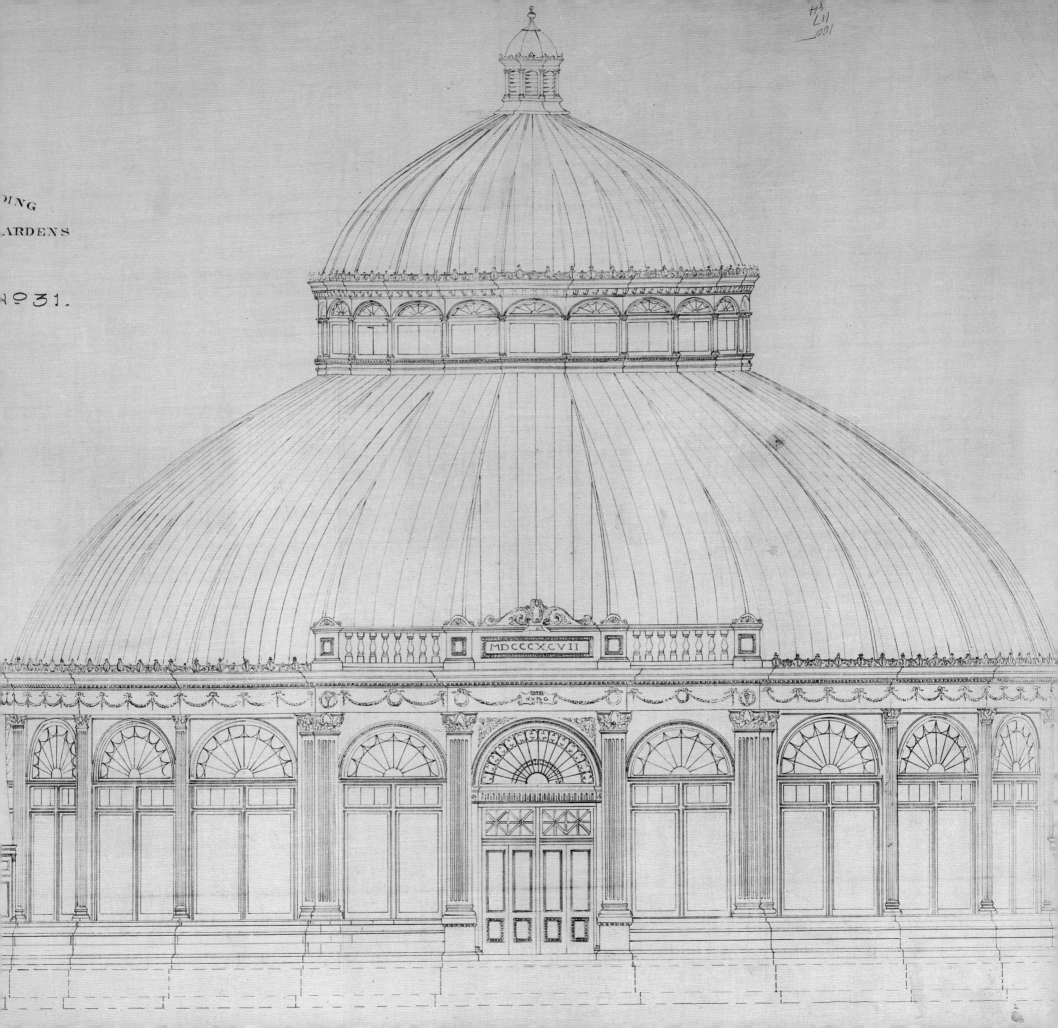

MDCCCXCVII

NOTABLE ARCHITECTURE   GREGORY LONG

A remarkable collection of historic and notable buildings can be seen among the rolling hills and dales, the ancient rock outcrops, and the thousands of noble trees of the New York Botanical Garden's nineteenth-century landscape. A walk or a ride on the tram around the Garden is almost as rewarding for the architecture as it is for the plants. This museum of plants is also, in a subtle way, a museum of American architecture.

FIRST BUILDINGS

The Garden's architectural story begins with the fieldstone buildings erected here in the first half of the nineteenth century by brothers Peter and George Lorillard. This French Huguenot family was in the tobacco business, and in 1792 they moved their industrial operations to the Bronx because of the water power available from the rushing Bronx River. The Lorillards raised tobacco in Connecticut, and their business was based in Manhattan, but they came to this site to build a large mill.

Their first building has not survived, but the current Snuff Mill, one of New York City's most picturesque remaining pre-Civil War industrial buildings, was built about 1840 to manufacture snuff for the European market. In the 1850s, the Lorillards constructed three other buildings nearby: an Italianate mansion, which was destroyed by fire in 1923; the extant Gothic Revival stone cottage overlooking the Rose Garden; and the stable, now a service building for the Garden and not on public view. These early buildings are built of stone called Fordham gneiss, which is closely related to Manhattan schist, the stone base of Manhattan Island. The doors and window openings are surrounded by brick. The Snuff Mill has been designated both a New York City Landmark and a National Historic Landmark. Having fallen into disrepair, the much-loved building was restored in 1950 and a respectful face-lift is scheduled for 2006.

PREVIOUS SPREAD

An original drawing of the façade of the Enid A. Haupt Conservatory by the designers and builders Lord & Burnham

ABOVE

The river front of the Snuff Mill can be seen in this watercolor rendering painted by Thomas Schaller about 1995.

RIGHT

Known as the Stone Cottage, this small building functioned as a gate house on the Lorillard estate.

THE BOTANICAL GARDEN ARRIVES: THE GREAT CONSERVATORY

The next buildings erected on the site were those created by the founders in the 1890s, when the New York Botanical Garden was established. The great Conservatory, which was completed in 1902, is still the centerpiece of the institution, the icon around which all subsequent buildings are organized, and the one to which they pay homage. As one member of the Garden's current governing body puts it: "Glass is us." The Conservatory is the preeminent existing American example of the crystal palace glass-and-steel school of design developed in England and Ireland in the mid-nineteenth century. The building was high-tech at the time of its creation by the architect William R. Cobb and the famous greenhouse firm Lord & Burnham. Lord & Burnham made a tremendous name for itself by constructing palatial glass-and-steel conservatories like this for American tycoons and botanical gardens (Buffalo, Pittsburgh, San Francisco) during the so-called American Renaissance, the period of fabulous wealth between the Civil War and World War I. The Garden's Conservatory has always been a status symbol and is so even today. It is an entire acre under glass, and the dome rises ninety feet in height. The symmetrical plan is "C"-shaped, with long, rectangular courtyards and reflecting pools enclosed by embracing arms. The building is four hundred feet long and contains seventeen thousand panes of glass, most of them curved and custom manufactured; all of the windows were replaced during the significant restoration of 1994–97 by the New York architectural firm Beyer Blinder Belle.

The southwest façade of the
Conservatory, resting on its
formal plinth, in a photograph
from one hundred years ago

Most of the classical details of the Conservatory are rendered in cast iron and pressed metal. Deteriorated structural elements were replaced with more durable materials during the major restoration in 1994–97.

There are two principal hills in the northern section of the Garden—one is crowned by the formal Beaux-Arts precinct surrounding the Conservatory and the other is surmounted by the brick, limestone, and terra-cotta Library building created by Robert Gibson in 1901. Reminiscent of a Roman Baroque palace, this massive masonry structure, a turn-of-the-century "civic monument," sits at the head of the majestic double allée of tulip trees planted here by Garden cofounder Nathaniel Lord Britton. The building is capped with a green copper dome almost as beautiful as the Conservatory's glass dome two thousand feet away on the other hilltop. The Library building symbolizes the academic and intellectual mission of the Garden, just as the Conservatory embodies public education and the enjoyment of plants.

In the overall picturesque, or naturalistic, style of the Garden's landscape design, the two formal areas created to frame the two principal buildings are the Library's Italianate tulip tree formation and the raised platform on which the Conservatory rests. The tulip trees are accompanied by the majestic Beaux-Arts fountain at the head of the tulip tree walks and just below the giant Corinthian limestone columns of the main entrance to the building. Now known as the Lillian Goldman Fountain of Life, the figures and the basins are by the sculptor Charles E. Tefft. Inspired by the Baroque fountains of Rome, the newly restored fountain was rededicated in 2005.

A blueprint by Robert Gibson
of the principal façade of the
Library building

In this spectacular photograph of the Library building after the restoration in 2002, the antique copper and glass dome of the rotunda glows against the night sky.

Other noteworthy structures from the period of the founders include several massive stone bridges that support roads across the Bronx River, dating variously from 1900 to 1950, as well as another lovely span across Twin Lakes and the pedestrian high bridge, which also crosses the river. The pedestrian bridge is now known as Hester Bridge, named for the Garden's sixth president, James Hester (1980–89). It is perched 150 feet above the river, where it joins the two parts of the native forest. The fact that these bridges had to be installed early in the twentieth century is a reminder that this landscape was virgin forest and rough farmland before the New York Botanical Garden was established, and that the task of creating the institution was massive and on an almost imperial scale.

RIGHT

The seals of the New York Botanical Garden (top), United States (left), New York City (center), and New York State (right) decorate the façade of the Library building.

OPPOSITE

Designed by the American Renaissance sculptor Charles E. Tefft, the Lillian Goldman Fountain of Life is a dramatic composition featuring sea nymphs, seahorses, cherubs, and a startled mermaid and merman. The water falls into two basins of white marble.

OPPOSITE ABOVE
Originally known as High
Bridge, now as Hester Bridge,
this camel-back structure high
above the Bronx River was
constructed nearly one hundred
years ago.

OPPOSITE LEFT
Built in 1907, Long Bridge still
carries traffic around the northern perimeter of the Garden.

OPPOSITE CENTER
Linnaean Bridge, shown in 1910,
crosses the Bronx River at the
southern end of the Garden.

OPPOSITE RIGHT
Upper Bridge, built in 1906
amid native flora, is reflected
in the Bronx River. It has
since been replaced with a mid-
twentieth-century structure.

ABOVE
Snuff Mill Bridge was built
in 1950.

NEW BUILDINGS

Beginning in the 1990s, a renewed commitment to excellence by the leadership of the Garden led to a new wave of building, which is now nearing its conclusion. At the side of the Library building, Susan T. Rodriquez and James Polshek, partners in the New York architectural firm Polshek Partnership Architects, created a new structure for the housing of the Library stacks and the Herbarium. Dedicated in 2002, this 70,000-square-foot building will have a green wall of vines as its principal façade when the Virginia creeper, now making its way up the wall, reaches maturity.

At Conservatory Gate, the main entrance to the Garden, Hugh Hardy of the New York firm H³ Hardy Collaboration Architecture designed a cluster of low glass, stone, and steel buildings. Opened in 2004, the Leon Levy Visitor Center is stylistically mid-twentieth-century modern in inspiration, but it blends seamlessly with the historic landscape and the Conifer Arboretum in which it is set.

Positioned, like the Visitor Center, near the Conservatory is a pink brick structure housing the Garden Cafe and the Garden Terrace Room. The building, designed by Jaquelin T. Robertson of the New York firm Cooper, Robertson & Partners, is sunk elegantly into a hilltop in order to make it subordinate and respectful to the northeast corner of the Conservatory, which is not far away.

OPPOSITE
Resting on a level platform of turf, the bookstore and retail facility exemplifies the Garden's theme of elegant glass construction.

LEFT
A Thomas Schaller rendering of the entrance to the Garden Cafe designed by Cooper, Robertson & Partners in 1997

OPPOSITE
High-tech in the extreme, the new greenhouses are principally for behind-the-scenes propagation, but they are also a stop for visitors on the Garden tram tour.

ABOVE
The Bourke-Sullivan Display House filled to the brim with auricula primroses, hanging baskets of fuchsia, and sweetly scented heliotrope

LEFT
Auricula primroses, with their painted porcelain-like flowers, are sometimes exhibited in the Bourke-Sullivan Display House of the Nolen Greenhouses.

The Nolen Greenhouses for Living Collections are located diagonally across the landscape of the Garden. This facility, which includes the Bourke-Sullivan Display House, was dedicated in 2005. Jan Keane and James Braddock of New York-based Mitchell/Giurgola Architects designed the complex, and the Van Wingerden Greenhouse Company provided the glass and steel components. These houses, which cover a full acre, are where the staff grow and study the Garden's plant collections. The most notable feature of these very high-tech buildings is that their pitched roofs are capable of opening up completely, so that each leaf of the roof stands up from the building at a 90-degree angle. This computer-controlled feature allows for high-quality horticulture and plant production. A monumental bronze sculpture by Tom Otterness of the four life stages of the remarkable plant titan arum (*Amorphophallus titanum*) is installed at the entrance to the Nolen Greenhouses.

The Everett Children's Adventure Garden, teaching children about plants, was built in the late 1990s. This fifteen-acre garden within the Garden was designed by the architectural firm of Richard L. Dattner. The buildings are playful adaptations of late nineteenth-century Adirondack cottages.

Charming additions to the Garden in the past generation include the fences and gazebo of the Peggy Rockefeller Rose Garden, which were designed in 1916 but not constructed until the 1980s. Three stone pavilions nearby, designed by Marian Cruger Coffin in the 1940s but not built at that time, have recently been installed as part of the restoration of the historic Benenson Ornamental Conifers.

LEFT
The celebrated garden designer Beatrix Jones Farrand intended the gazebo and fence of the Rose Garden to be made of wood, but when they were constructed in 1988, seventy-two years later, they were wisely built of steel.

OPPOSITE
Marian Cruger Coffin, most famous for her design of the gardens at Winterthur in Delaware, envisioned this pair of stone pavilions for the entrance to the ornamental conifer collection in the 1940s, but they were not built in this position until 2004.

THE RESEARCH

EX HERBARIO MUSEI BRITANNICI

PLANTS OF
CAPTAIN COOK'S FIRST VOYAGE
1768-1771

Chiliotrichum amelloides Cass.

TIERRA DEL FUEGO

15-21.i.1769

Coll. Joseph Banks & Daniel Solander

SEVEN MILLION SPECIMENS AND COUNTING
THE WILLIAM AND LYNDA STEERE HERBARIUM
BARBARA M. THIERS

EARLY SPECIMENS

The New York Botanical Garden's Herbarium, a reference collection of 7.2 million dried plant and fungal specimens for research use, was an important resource on the day it opened in 1901. Immediately after the Garden's incorporation in 1891, Nathaniel Lord Britton, its founding director, had begun actively acquiring specimens for a herbarium. Particularly noteworthy among these early holdings was the Torrey Herbarium, perhaps the most comprehensive collection of American plant specimens at the time. John Torrey (1796–1873), the first internationally renowned American botanist, received plant specimens such as those collected on John C. Frémont's exploring expeditions in 1842–45 to the Oregon Territory and California and the surveys in 1853–55 for the Pacific Railroad routes. The private herbarium of Job Bicknell Ellis (1829–1905), which included more than four thousand species previously unknown to European scientists, was also among the outstanding original acquisitions. A New Jersey native, Ellis was the first to document the fungi responsible for diseases of crop and ornamental plants in the Western Hemisphere.

Building on this impressive foundation, the Garden's Herbarium grew quickly in size and depth, and by 1934, it contained nearly two million specimens. Vigorous collecting programs carried out by Garden scientists throughout the Western Hemisphere were the source of many of these early collections, which also included specimen-exchange programs with the Smithsonian Institution, Harvard University, Royal Botanic Gardens, Kew, and St. Petersburg Botanical Garden in Russia, among others. The herbarium of William Mitten, a British apothecary and eminent amateur botanist, was purchased by the Garden from his family, an acquisition that contributed 50,000 specimens of mosses and related plants collected during the most important British expeditions—from Captain Cook's exploration of the South Pacific to Charles Darwin's voyage aboard H.M. discovery ship *Beagle*.

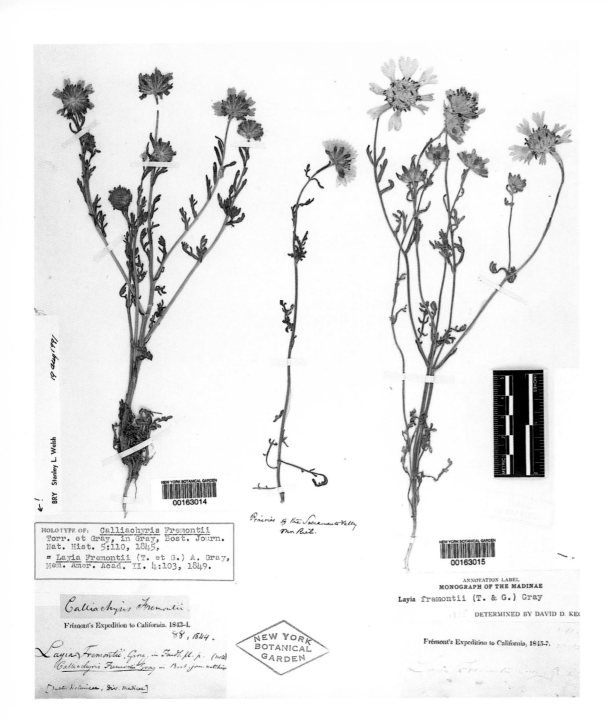

PREVIOUS SPREAD

During Captain James Cook's first voyage to the Pacific in 1768–71, his shipboard botanists collected many plant specimens, most of which are in the British Museum. The Garden acquired this Cook specimen by exchange with the museum.

LEFT

When John C. Frémont was exploring Oregon and California, he collected plants to document the biodiversity of this newly opened part of America, and many of these specimens reside in the Steere Herbarium.

ABOVE

During General William Custer's 1874 expedition to the Black Hills, botanists accompanying him found this flowering shrub in South Dakota.

TYPE SPECIMENS

Herbarium specimens document the vegetation on Earth, past and present, and each one of the 7.2 million specimens in the Garden's Herbarium contributes to that documentation. Some specimens, known as "type" specimens, have added importance because they were selected to serve as standards for the name of a plant species. The rules of botanical nomenclature dictate that for every new species of plant that is described, one specimen must be designated as its type. This designation is permanent, and any thorough characterization of a plant species requires reference to the type specimen. For this reason, access to type specimens is critically important for studying plant diversity, and these specimens are the most frequently consulted holdings of any herbarium.

The William and Lynda Steere Herbarium (named for the son and daughter-in-law of Dr. William Campbell Steere, who led the Garden from 1958 to 1972) has approximately 150,000 type specimens of plants and fungi, many of them found in the original herbaria acquired soon after the Garden was founded. These document some of the earliest botanical studies conducted in North America. The types most frequently consulted, however, are the more than 13,000 species that have been described by Garden scientists. The Garden is particularly well known for its type specimens of the sunflower, bean, and coffee families.

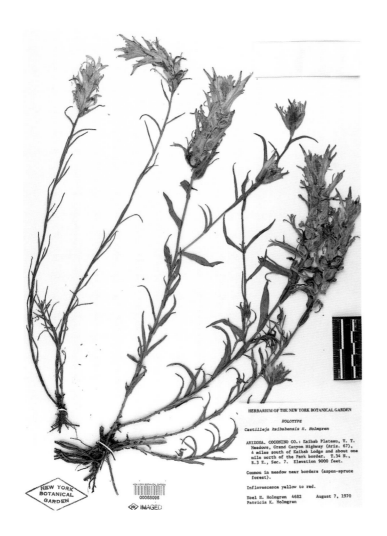

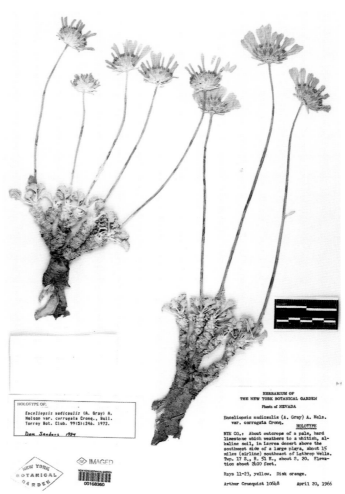

Two "type" specimens from the Steere Herbarium, both small flowering plants from the western United States

The Garden's Herbarium continues to grow at a rate of 50,000 to 75,000 specimens a year, keeping pace with the rate of acquisition throughout its history. The sources of new accessions today are similar to those of the early years—staff expeditions, exchange programs with other herbaria, gifts sent to Garden scientists in return for identification, and purchases.

Recent advances in technology have allowed information gathering on field expeditions to become more comprehensive and precise than during previous periods. In the earliest collecting expeditions, Garden scientists were often accompanied by artists, who would sketch and paint the specimens as they were collected. They recorded information in notebooks, and, owing to a paucity of maps, sometimes described collecting locations in terms of length of time it took to walk or ride a horse from the nearest town. Today scientists plan expeditions using databases and satellite images to locate collection sites, and they frequently travel by jeep or helicopter, equipped with digital cameras and laptop computers to record information from collections as they are gathered. They pinpoint collection sites using geographical coordinates determined by hand-held global positioning devices, and they prepare samples for molecular analysis back in the laboratory. As a result, recent collections can be more completely characterized than was previously possible.

FAR LEFT
A highly decorative herbarium specimen of a small penstemon found in the arid landscape of the American West

LEFT
In this tropical blueberry plant specimen, the leaves, once green, have faded to brown.

PROCESSING FIELD COLLECTIONS

New York Botanical Garden scientists collect specimens to document the biodiversity of a particular region (a floristic study or flora) or to analyze the variations within a particular group of plants or fungi (a monographic study or monograph). Sometimes collections document important biological relationships between organisms, such as pollinator-flower relationships. Ethnobotanists also make herbarium collections of plants used by people for food, medicine, ceremony, or shelter.

Field collection involves removing a representative portion of the organism, recording information about it, and then preserving it. The time-honored tool for preserving collections is the plant press, in which samples are sandwiched between layers of absorbent paper, bound tightly, and placed over a heat source. Wherever possible, Garden field scientists collect specimens in multiple sets; the first set is always deposited in a local herbarium for the benefit of local plant biodiversity studies and the training of future regional botanists, and the second set is deposited in the Steere Herbarium. Duplicate sets will also be shared with other institutions, offered as a gift in return for an expert identification, or as an exchange. Exchange programs allow many herbaria to be enriched from a single collecting expedition.

For deposition in the Herbarium, specimens are typically glued to stiff sheets of paper, while bulkier organisms are placed in cardboard boxes. The collection documentation is transcribed into the Garden's Virtual Herbarium, from which a specimen label is printed and affixed to the specimen sheet or box. A completed specimen is filed in specially designed steel cabinets, arranged by family, genus, species, and the geographical region of the world where it was collected.

A herbarium specimen is fashioned from a portion of a plant (ideally including leaves, stems, and flowers) that is pressed and dried immediately upon collection.

VIRTUAL HERBARIUM

For most of the Herbarium's history, the only way to know what specimens it contained was to look at the specimens themselves. To make the content more accessible, the Garden embarked in 1995 upon the monumental task of creating an electronic catalogue of the Herbarium. Today this catalogue contains approximately 800,000 specimen entries, as well as high-quality digital images that anyone in the world can access through the Virtual Herbarium on the Garden's Web site (www.nybg.org). Data from the Virtual Herbarium can be used not only for floras and monographs, but may also be incorporated into broad-scale geographical analyses to identify factors that influence what organisms grow where, and to predict what effects human-induced changes may have on the environment.

Although cataloguing the entire Steere Herbarium will take many years, several important subsets have already been completed. The Garden was the first of the world's major herbaria to catalogue and reproduce images of all its type specimens of flowering plants (about 100,000 specimens and images) and is the first to finish cataloguing the bryophytes (mosses and related species, about 300,000 specimens) for the North American continent. Also completed is a catalogue of the plants of the eastern states of Brazil, where environmental threat to natural areas is high. In addition to specimen data, the Virtual Herbarium includes *Index Herbariorum,* a directory of the world's herbaria, and *Index to American Botanical Literature,* a comprehensive bibliography for the plants and fungi of the New World.

Garden scientists collect every kind of plant. In this West Virginia landscape, William T. Buck, Ph.D., examines and collects mosses and lichens for herbarium specimens, which will also be digitized for the Virtual Herbarium.

ryllis Josephinæ.

214

Amaryllis de J.

A TREASURY OF BOTANICAL KNOWLEDGE
THE LuESTHER T. MERTZ LIBRARY
SUSAN FRASER

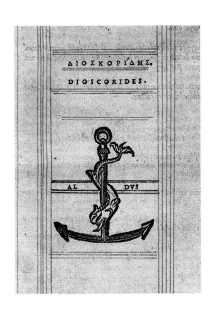

BOTANY AND HORTICULTURE: THE HISTORICAL RECORD

The LuEsther T. Mertz Library of the New York Botanical Garden houses published and archival documents that trace the development of botany and horticulture from the twelfth century to the present day—from their origins in ancient medicine and agriculture to the most modern advances in plant molecular biology. It is now the world's largest and most active botanical and horticultural Library, with collections comprising more than one million items. Among the riches is an excellent representation of the important pioneering botanical and horticultural works published in Europe and America over the past five hundred years. Other areas of collection strength are systematic, floristic, and economic botany and horticulture, gardening, and landscape design. These subjects are reflected not only in the large collection of books and journals, but also in electronic databases, nursery catalogues, manuscripts, prints and drawings, and scientific reprints.

Both a scholarly resource and a public research center for information about plants, the Library also provides online access to digitized books, electronic journals, and searchable databases, which contain the latest results of research and discovery in plant science and modern horticultural practice.

The oldest work in the collection is a twelfth-century manuscript of the *Circa instans*, one of the earliest surviving copies of a treatise that originated at Europe's first medical school in Salerno, Italy. The treatise is attributed to Matthaeus Platerius, one of the school's foremost teaching physicians, and is the prototype of both the modern pharmacopoeia and the herbal. It comprises a list of "simples," or primary ingredients, from which compound prescriptions were formulated. In this and other early herbals, the emphasis is on the medicinal virtues or properties of plants in their relationship to man, rather than botanical information.

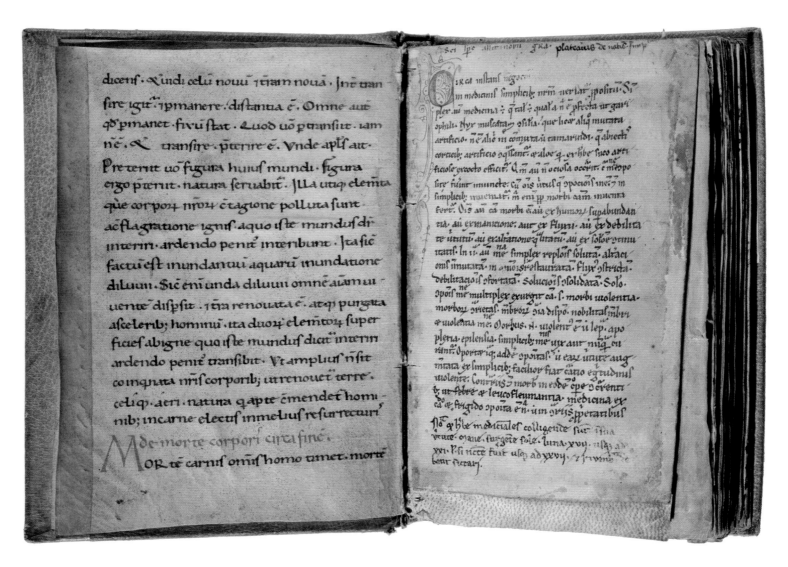

PAGE 214

Among the Library's greatest illustrated books, few are more spectacular than *Les Liliacées* by Pierre-Joseph Redouté. This is the only double-page plate from this monumental eight-volume work.

PAGE 215

Although Dioscorides wrote his books about medicinal plants and minerals in the first century A.D., this edition was published in Venice by the distinguished Aldine Press 1,500 years later. The anchor-and-dolphin device is the colophon of the Aldine Press.

ABOVE

Circa instans is a medieval manuscript on vellum, c. 1190.

The Library owns later editions of many landmark works, including one of the earliest attempts at botanical classification, *De historia plantarum*, by Theophrastus (c. 371–c. 287 B.C.), a pupil of Aristotle, published in 1522. Another important early work is *De medica materia*, the precursor of all modern pharmacopeias. It was written by Pedanius Dioscorides (c. 40–c. 90 A.D.), a celebrated Greek physician, botanist, pharmacologist, and surgeon. A compilation of knowledge augmented by the author's own observations and experiences during his travels with the armies of the Roman emperor Nero, it established the basis for all subsequent herbal literature after its publication in 1529. Many of the early herbals are considered milestones in the history of printing and scientific illustration, but these published works were simply copies of early

Printed in Augsburg in 1475, this early treatise is illustrated with hand-colored woodcuts of plants.

manuscripts, complete with unsubstantiated information and crude illustrations. Using the same plates to illustrate different books was common in herbals throughout the sixteenth century and into the seventeenth. An exception was Otto Brunfels's 1530 publication of *Herbarium Vivae Eicones* (Living Portraits of Plants) in which the illustrations were based on the actual observation of the plant. His book helped put an end to the tradition of copying from other illustrations or reusing existing woodblocks.

The pasque flower, which is still cultivated in our gardens today, was accurately depicted in the Renaissance herbal of Otto Brunfels.

SUMPTUOUS PLATE BOOKS

Increasingly detailed and accurate illustrations were an essential part of the eighteenth- and nineteenth-century movement toward scientific botany. As improvements were made in travel and navigation, scientific expeditions were undertaken with increasing frequency. Expeditions in pursuit of new geographical information expanded to include significant plant collection. It was not uncommon for these expeditions to include an artist who would illustrate plants that were discovered and collected, and for the findings to be published in sumptuously illustrated volumes. In many countries, private patronage and official court flower painters were responsible for commissions of some of the most notable flower books ever created.

In this lavish, hand-colored chromolithograph from a nineteenth-century German publication by Karl Friedrich Philipp von Martius, well-dressed botanist Eduard Poeppig is shown pressing a specimen, accompanied by his faithful dog.

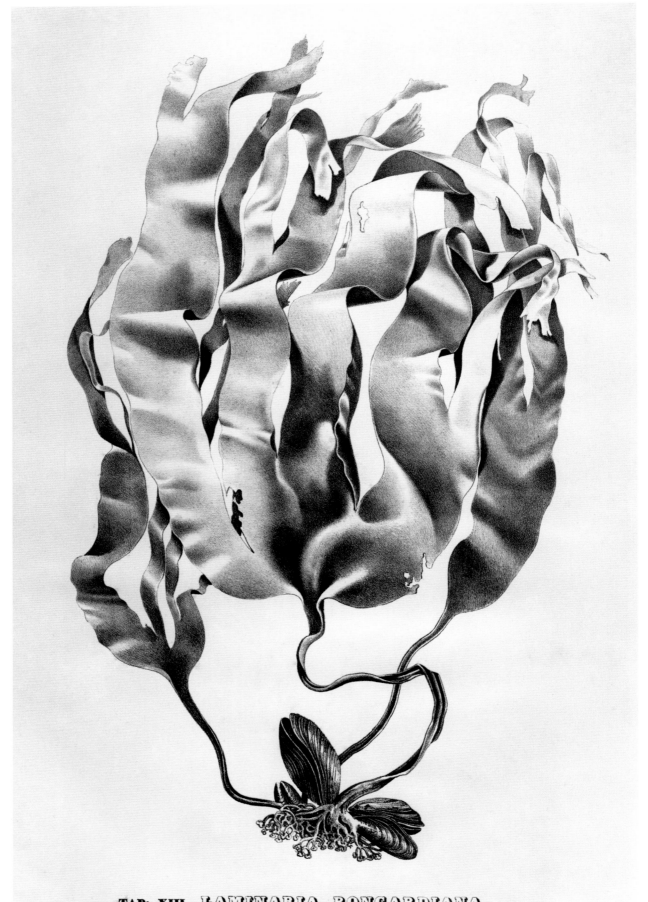

TAB: XIII. LAMINARIA BONGARDIANA *palmata.*

From about 1600 to 1850, the illustrations in many natural-history books were produced from copperplate engravings and colored by hand. The Dutch, German, English, and French led the field in the production of these magnificent tomes. Although many of the drawings were made in the service of botany, their exquisite execution and intrinsic beauty make them works of art as well as science. The Library's collections include thousands of large-format, illustrated plate books, which began to be amassed in the 1890s by members of the Garden's board of managers, among them J. P. Morgan and Andrew Carnegie. Two stellar examples are *Plantae Selectae* and *Hortus Nitidisimus,* which were illustrated by Georg Dionysius Ehret and published by Christoph Jacob Trew, a wealthy Nuremberg physician who sponsored Ehret's travels and commissioned many of his drawings. The hand-colored engravings of Ehret's plant portraits made him one of the most highly regarded botanical illustrators of the era. Another famous example came from France where, under the patronage of Empress Joséphine Bonaparte, Pierre-Joseph Redouté, a French artist of Flemish origin, painted the flowers in her garden at Malmaison. Over many years, Redouté created beautiful watercolors for several botanical works, including *Les Roses,* which depicted many of the nearly 250 varieties of roses that thrived at Joséphine's country estate.

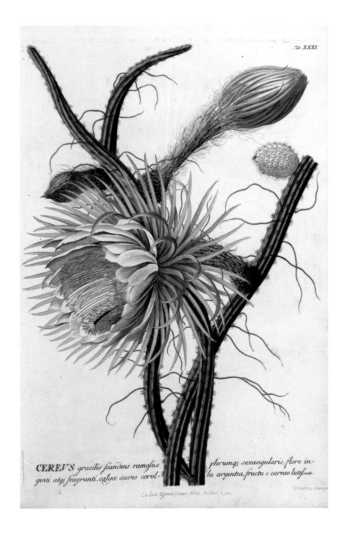

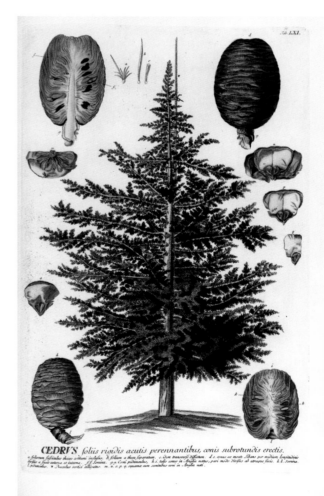

ELIZABETH KALS REILLEY COLLECTION

One of the finest private collections of rare garden books ever assembled was given to the New York Botanical Garden in 2002 by the collector Elizabeth Kals Reilley, a connoisseur, bibliophile, and professional librarian. Many of the books, engravings, and other printed materials relating to the early development of garden design in Europe date back to the Renaissance. Among the Reilley collection treasures are *Trattato della agricoltura . . .* , the fundamental horticultural manual of the sixteenth century, by Pietro di Crescenzi (1784); the first book of French garden

An eighteenth-century Austrian
garden design book by Salomon
Kleiner depicts an elaborate
topiary garden.

LEFT

A rare seventeenth-century engraving by Stefano della Bella illustrating the Colossal Statue of the Apennines in the Medici garden at Pratolino

BELOW LEFT

The frontpiece from Giovanni Battista Falda's 1683 survey, *The Gardens of Rome*

designs, by Jacques Androuet du Cerceau (1576); the first book of garden patterns, by Flemish designer Hans Vredeman de Vries (1583); seminal Renaissance works in architecture and garden design by Vitruvius, Alberti, and Palladio; the book of flower portraits that launched the notorious "tulipomania" of the early seventeenth century; the work that codified French garden design in the style of André Le Nôtre; and the leading treatises and published views of English landscape garden design and the picturesque movement. Crowning the Reilley collection is an exceptionally rare "Red Book" by Humphry Repton, a watercolor and manuscript proposal for new landscape designs for the estate at Whitton in Middlesex, England. This unique and comprehensive collection enriches the Garden's collections and makes the Mertz Library an essential scholarly resource for the appreciation and study of landscape design history.

A watercolor illustration by Humphry Repton from his "Red Book," presenting a redesign for the garden and park at Whitton, the seat of Samuel Prime, Esq.

In 2002 David L. Andrews, M.D., then chairman of the Library Visiting Committee, announced his plans to donate his extensive Library to the Garden. This superb collection of thousands of books and ephemera records the history of the exploration, classification, and development of America's botanical riches. In donating his collection, Dr. Andrews continued the tradition of other great benefactors who have played key roles in solidifying the Garden's position as a major international botanical and horticultural research center.

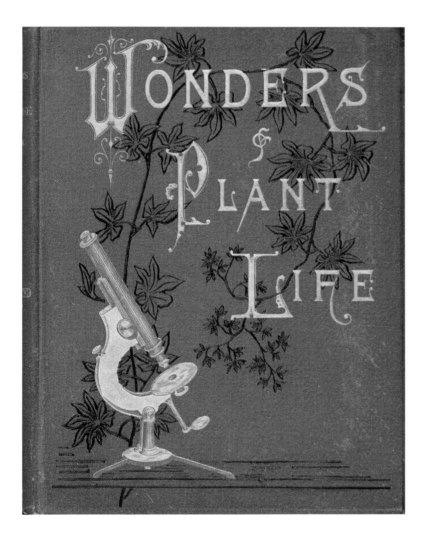

FAR LEFT
The Andrews collection contains many examples of ornamental gold-stamp bindings from the mid-nineteenth century.

LEFT
The king of the Seminoles was illustrated in William Bartam's 1791 *Travels through North & South Carolina, Georgia, East & West Florida.*

Early European exploration of America and the emerging American scientific and horticultural community that studied and developed the nation's natural resources are chronicled through their published works. The continuing pursuit of scientific understanding in plant studies produced a wealth of information that documents the history of American botany in print. A fascination with imported European fruits and their subsequent American hybridization is explored through books and prints, including quintessentially American "how to" books on fruits, flowers, and kitchen gardens. The emergence of nurseries and their advertising practices is documented in early letterpress catalogues and nurserymen's plate books. In the nineteenth century, nursery catalogues evolved from simple seed and plant lists to colorful illustrated advertising tools that took full advantage of increasingly sophisticated printing techniques.

FLOWERS FROM SEEDS

MISS C·H·LIPPINCOTT
319 & 323 Sixth St. S. MINNEAPOLIS MINN.

OPPOSITE

An eighteenth-century engraving depicting native people and plants of North America at the moment of discovery by European voyagers

LEFT

The cover of a late-nineteenth-century seed catalogue, one of hundreds in the Andrews collection

BELOW LEFT

The American black oak as illustrated in François Michaux's 1817 treatise on the trees of North America

BELOW CENTER

The title page of *The New England Book of Fruits* by John M. Ives, 1847

BELOW RIGHT

An original watercolor by Joseph B. Prestele from a set of fruit paintings, c. 1850

Black Oak.
Quercus tinctoria.

THE
New England
BOOK OF FRUITS
Containing the
APPLE, PEAR, PEACH, PLUM, CHERRY, GRAPE &c.
BY
JOHN M. IVES.

SALEM.
W. & S. B. IVES, PUBLISHERS.
1847.

Early Joe Apple.

227

BOTANICAL ART AND ILLUSTRATION

The Library's Art and Illustration Collection is an important tool for basic research. It is also a valuable and useful resource in the history of botanical art for the scholarly comparison of originals to published work and for exhibitions. The collection contains more than 22,000 original works in an assortment of media, including line drawings, watercolors, oil paintings, woodcuts, lithographs, engravings, and sculpture. It represents the broad range of illustrative techniques employed in depicting natural history. Many of the works in the collection are by noted artists and were produced with the finest printing techniques available. A fairly complete history of fine printing techniques could be assembled using the illustrations found in this collection.

Many of these works are by distinguished artists, including the Garden's former staff artists. Among them are the pen-and-ink line drawings, the principal means of identification of plant species in scientific publications, of Auguste Mariolle, botanical artist for the Université de Marseilles from 1892 to 1901 and staff artist for the Garden from 1901 to 1911; the botanical watercolors of Mary Eaton, staff artist from 1911 to 1932 and principal illustrator for the Garden's illustrated serial *Addisonia* and Britton and Rose's *The Cactaceae* (1919–23); as well as many research drawings made by talented Works Progress Administration artists during the Great Depression.

In 1910, a gift of pencil drawings from Professor D. N. Martin included sketches of the structure of the flower and fruit of New York State plants by early American botanist John Torrey. Other drawings by Torrey and by Isaac Sprague and Arthur Schott, who served as artists on several government-sponsored expeditions and surveys, were the gifts of Mrs. Addison Brown from her husband's collection. In 1914, an exchange of material from the Berlin Botanic Garden produced a collection of more than three hundred original drawings from *Flora Brasiliensis* by Karl F. P. von Martius. Frances Horne donated a collection of about seven hundred watercolors of the plants of Puerto Rico, which she prepared to accompany Nathaniel Lord Britton's *Flora Borinquena*; and Anne Ophelia Dowden deposited more than six hundred detailed research paintings prepared from observing living plants, all studies for her finished paintings.

EXHIBITIONS

The William D. Rondina and Giovanni Foroni LoFaro Gallery, designed by Stephen Saitas, opened in May 2002. It is a 900-square-foot venue for exhibitions that highlight rare, beautiful, and historically important works from the Garden's extensive collections. Because preservation of the valuable collections is critically important, the gallery is equipped with controls that record the hourly temperature and relative humidity and regulate as necessary, in addition to a security system with closed-circuit television for monitoring. The Library presents two museum-quality exhibitions in the gallery each year, accompanied by scholarly publications.

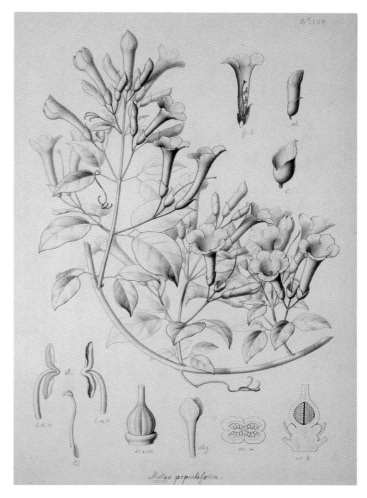

A watercolor drawing of colorful mushrooms by the botanical
artist Mary E. Eaton, c. 1930

A pencil drawing done for von
Martius, part of a large set of
drawings in the Library, produced for his immense survey
of the plants of Brazil

FROM THE BRONX TO BORNEO: THE INTERNATIONAL PLANT SCIENCE CENTER

The New York Botanical Garden's act of incorporation, dated April 28, 1891, called for "the advancement of botanical science and knowledge and the prosecution of original researches therein." Today, more than two hundred Ph.D. scientists, graduate students, and technical staff based at the Garden keep this proud tradition thriving. They are linked with hundreds of colleagues at other gardens, museums, universities, non-governmental organizations, and governments worldwide. Since 2000 all of their complex activity has been organized into the Garden's International Plant Science Center (IPSC).

The IPSC encompasses the outstanding collections of the William and Lynda Steere Herbarium and the LuEsther T. Mertz Library; other components are the Institute of Systematic Botany, Institute of Economic Botany, Lewis B. and Dorothy Cullman Program for Molecular Systematics Studies, and Genomics Program, which includes the New York Plant Genomics Consortium. Many of the studies by scientists in these units are conducted in the Garden's new Pfizer Plant Research Laboratory. The science center's educational mission is carried out through its distinguished graduate studies program. Since research is not complete until it is published, the science center includes the New York Botanical Garden Press for the dissemination of research results.

James Luteyn, Ph.D., collects plants in the high Andes of Ecuador.

FIELD BIOLOGY

Most activities of the IPSC begin, and in some cases also end, in the field, from as close to home as an oak-maple forest in the Bronx to such far-flung places as a rain forest in Borneo. The Garden is internationally renowned for its field programs, having conducted since 1897 more than two thousand plant collecting expeditions or on-site projects in the United States and abroad, in as many as one hundred different countries.

Some field biology consists of straightforward plant exploration, which involves the documentation of an organism's existence in a certain place at a certain time and then the collection of specimens or samples of the organisms encountered on the expedition. This activity is an essential first step toward other more complex studies of plant ecology, evolution, and conservation. An excellent example of important plant exploration was Projeto Flora Amazónica, a collaboration between the New York Botanical Garden and the Brazilian government that involved forty-six expeditions in the 1970s and 1980s, during which 73,000 plant specimens were collected.

Plant exploration of the Amazon continues to be a major area of activity for the Garden. Its current geographic focus is southwestern Amazonia, the most remote and least-known sector of the region. There, modern collecting techniques and sophisticated technologies are employed to improve the value and information content of the collections. In Acre, Brazil, Garden scientists have collected thousands of specimens since 1990 and are using the resulting data to influence environmental policy. They do this by helping Brazilian environmental policymakers devise land-use management plans that promote long-term biodiversity conservation and sustainable development.

One of the key tools used by the Garden to further these conservation efforts is the production of floras, which are detailed and in-depth descriptions of the plant diversity of a geographic region. Over the past

century in the United States, for example, the Garden has produced floras for vast sections of the western, southeastern, and northeastern regions of the country. *Intermountain Flora*, which is projected to be a six-volume series, covers all of Utah, major parts of Nevada and Idaho, and areas of Oregon, California, Arizona, and Wyoming. An indispensable work of reference, it is widely used by conservationists and land-use managers for conservation efforts throughout the western United States.

Another example is the result of a quarter-century-long initiative led by Garden scientists in French Guiana. Involving innumerable expeditions, resulting in tens of thousands of plant collections, this in-depth study of the plants of a 346,418-acre area around the village of Saül has made this the best botanically known tract of lowland rain forest in South America.

Systematic biology field work can also result in a monographic study, which presents a synthesis of everything that is known about a group of organisms, such as a genus or family of plants, wherever the group occurs in the world. One example is field work that is being carried out on the blueberry family in the New World tropics. In the field, many observations are made, for instance, of the pollinators and dispersers of the plants being studied. Specimens are collected for study in the Herbarium, and samples are often taken for subsequent DNA analysis in the laboratory. The result of years of such painstaking analysis and synthesis is a systematic biology monograph, the most authoritative source for information about a group of plants.

Studies that focus on the biology and classification of plants themselves constitute a large portion of the Garden's field efforts; the other major category of field work concerns the relationships between plants and people, the discipline known as economic botany. Economic botanists at the Garden study not only the value of plants as medicines, fuels, fibers, and foods,

but also how valuable plant resources can be managed in a sustainable way. Among the many examples that can be cited are studies conducted in Belize, Micronesia, Peru, and Brazil, and recently in Myanmar and Indonesia. Field studies in economic botany can often contribute to the conservation of biodiversity in managed and protected landscapes.

LABORATORIES

Plant specimens collected in the field are brought back to the Garden's science center for study. Much of this research takes place in the Steere Herbarium, but some is carried out in the laboratory. Laboratory study of plants at the Garden is not new. Historically, many areas have been explored, such as plant physiology, pathology, biochemistry, and genetics. IPSC lab facilities are housed in the Pfizer Plant Research Laboratory. Knowing the chemical components of plants is not only important for systematic botany studies, but also often vital in assessing the utility of plants. The laboratory has excellent capacity for extracting, purifying, and analyzing chemical compounds from plants.

The newest innovations to be added to the science center's "toolbox" come from molecular biology, specifically plant molecular systematics and genomics. In 1994 the Lewis B. and Dorothy Cullman Program for Molecular Systematics Studies was created in partnership with the American Museum of Natural History. For the first time, the Garden had the capacity to use DNA evidence in understanding the relationships among plants. Use of molecular data has now become routine, and IPSC researchers and their graduate students and collaborators are able to bring these powerful data to bear on important questions concerning plant classification, evolution, and conservation.

The most recent enhancement to the science center's laboratory occurred in 2000, when the Garden became a founding partner of the New York Plant Genomics Consortium, which has developed a model genomics program. The stature of this consortium was recognized by a major National Science Foundation grant in 2004 for a project that involves tracing the molecular relationship of cycads to higher seed plants in order to establish the evolution of seed development and discover genes with valuable agronomic traits. The findings are expected to open new windows on evolutionary questions within the plant kingdom. Equally important, the project itself is training a new class of biologists with interdisciplinary expertise in systematics and genomics.

GRADUATE STUDIES

The training of future generations of plant scientists has been a central mission of the New York Botanical Garden since it was founded. By 1900 the graduate studies program, then partnered with Columbia University, had grown to eight graduate students. Over the years, several hundred students from the United States and some two dozen other countries have received advanced degrees in many disciplines, including ecology, systematic botany, economic botany, plant physiology, phytochemistry, mycology, genetics, plant anatomy, paleobotany, and molecular systematics.

Garden scientists serve as advisors to the students, who enroll jointly with the Garden and with one of five participating universities—the City University of New York, Columbia University, Cornell University, New York University, and Yale University. Students take their course work through the universities and conduct their research under the direction of a Garden scientist. The Garden's graduate studies program, which currently enrolls an average of forty students a year, is internationally acclaimed for its success in preparing tomorrow's biodiversity researchers, since it offers comprehensive, broad-based practical experience through numerous research partnerships around the world.

PUBLICATIONS

The Garden's publishing program has disseminated scholarly information about plants and fungi and their conservation for more than a century. Today the New York Botanical Garden Press is the largest publishing program of any botanical garden in the world. It provides a primary publishing outlet for Garden scientists and their students, as well as colleagues at other institutions. The program is unrivaled in quality and productivity in the field of botanical science.

The press currently publishes three quarterly journals.

Brittonia, founded in 1931, is an important venue for publishing original results of systematic botany research. Since 1935 *The Botanical Review* has synthesized current knowledge about specific botanical topics and promoted their advancement by indicating gaps in our knowledge. *Economic Botany*, established in 1947, is an interdisciplinary journal concerned with the many and varied interrelationships between plants and people.

In addition to its journals, the press publishes five monographic series: *Contributions from The New York Botanical Garden* (1899–1933; 1984–present); *Memoirs of The New York Botanical Garden* (since 1900); *Flora Neotropica* (since 1968); *Intermountain Flora* (since 1972); and *Advances in Economic Botany* (since 1984).

The press has also published more than two hundred books that focus on the identification, classification, utilization, and conservation of plants and fungi. Among its classic, best-selling books are the *Illustrated Companion to Gleason and Cronquist's Manual of the Vascular Plants of Northeastern United States and Adjacent Canada*; *Biodiversity and Conservation of Neotropical Montane Forests*; *Floristic Inventory of Tropical Countries*; and *The Evolution and Classification of Flowering Plants*.

A TEACHING GARDEN

Although the New York Botanical Garden is internationally renowned for its work in botanical research, conservation, and horticultural technology and display, it plays an equally prominent and vitally important role closer to home. Since its establishment in 1891, the institution has been committed to serving the local community in a variety of ways. The Garden is a rare civic commodity—a historic natural topography preserved within one of the world's most complex urban centers. Over the years, its landscapes, collections, and programs have introduced generations of New Yorkers to the science, beauty, and variety of the plant world, enriching their lives and contributing to their understanding of Earth's great natural resources.

Today the Garden is a resource for the residents of the greater New York metropolitan region, providing programs and services that range from family activities to continuing education classes, plant information, and Library services. Its greatest impact, however, can be felt among its closest neighbors—the schoolchildren, educators, families, and citizens of the Bronx. In this large and diverse New York City borough, the Garden's 250 acres and nationally acclaimed children's education facilities function as an extension of public school classrooms and local backyards, while its outreach programs help communities transform urban eyesores into beautiful and productive green spaces. Professional development programs give city schoolteachers the tools they need to teach science effectively, while volunteer programs provide local youth with skill-building community service opportunities. The Garden is in partnership with elected officials,

New York City-area children learn to garden in the Ruth Rea Howell Family Garden.

school districts, and community representatives to continually assess and improve the services it offers to area residents.

EDUCATING NEW YORK CITY-AREA CHILDREN

The Garden is committed to improving scientific literacy and increasing young people's awareness of the value of plants and ecology. Its children's education program accomplishes this by offering innovative programming and by providing educators with resources that improve and enhance their teaching of science. For many inner-city children, the Garden offers a unique opportunity to experience nature firsthand and to engage in exploration and discovery, which lead to a deeper understanding of the living world.

233

The Everett Children's Adventure Garden is perhaps the best place in the world for children to learn plant science and ecology.

the Garden fills a critical gap, serving as an extension of the classroom and enhancing the opportunities for science education available to the Bronx school system. Several hundred thousand schoolchildren visit the adventure garden with their classes each year to experience guided explorations of the learning galleries by trained staff and volunteers. In addition, the Garden offers a teacher's guide, complete curriculum kits based on the adventure garden's facilities, and a range of onsite workshops, seminars, and weeklong summer institutes, where teachers can learn about plant science and inquiry-based teaching techniques.

The adventure garden's Intern Explainer Program is one of the Garden's after-school programs, which provide a safe and stimulating environment for urban youth. Middle and high school participants, primarily from Bronx schools, receive structured training before volunteering in the adventure garden, where they help younger children learn about science and nature.

CHILDREN LEARN TO GARDEN

The Ruth Rea Howell Family Garden is a one-and-a-half-acre walled garden where children learn to plant, tend, and harvest vegetables, flowers, and herbs. Although children's gardening has gained significant momentum in recent years, many New York City children have little access to the natural world, much less the opportunity to cultivate and tend plants themselves.

The family garden offers area children ages three to twelve the chance to learn gardening skills while nurturing a respect for and connection to nature. Through the children's gardening program, local youngsters care for individual garden plots over the course of one to three seasons, observing firsthand changes and growth from week to week. They also learn how to cook simple dishes from their freshly

Interactive facilities that capture young imaginations and foster curiosity are at the heart of the Garden's educational programs for children. Among these is the Everett Children's Adventure Garden, which was established in 1998. A twelve-acre, indoor-outdoor science museum, the adventure garden features four outdoor learning galleries, where children investigate plant anatomy, reproduction, and ecology while immersed in natural environments. Inside, a kids' laboratory and herbarium explain what plant scientists do and offer children a variety of hands-on activities. A five-acre urban wetland teeming with plant and wild-life borders the adventure garden,

offering lessons on ecology while encouraging observation and exploration.

Children who visit the adventure garden with their families engage in a wide range of activities and lessons that change throughout the year. Thematic programming introduces topics such as plant-animal interaction, seasonal changes, and everyday products that are derived from plants. These programs offer families an environment of educational fun in which parents and children together can learn about Earth's natural resources.

In a city in which schools are crowded, resources are limited, and many teachers lack science training,

harvested crops. City schoolchildren, primarily from the Bronx, also take advantage of the family garden through workshop series in which they learn about gardening, planting techniques, and composting.

Aside from structured programs, various informal learning activities are available to children and their families. Seasonal programming offers instruction on how to prepare a garden, plant seeds, make compost, pot up herbs, harvest vegetables, and winterize gardens. Multicultural programming highlights the diversity of the local community, featuring cultural crafts, cooking activities, and uses of plants.

BRONX GREEN-UP

Bronx Green-Up is the New York Botanical Garden's community gardening outreach program, established in 1988 as one of the first large-scale programs of its kind. Through it, Garden staff and volunteers provide horticultural training and resources that empower borough residents to reclaim and beautify their neighborhoods, while bringing communities together through urban greening projects. Since its establishment, the program has helped area groups create more than three hundred community gardens, transforming vacant, debris-filled lots into lush green spaces. Bronx Green-Up staff and volunteers offer bilingual workshops and horticultural training and distribute tools and plant materials, including thousands of seeds annually.

Seasonal events hosted by the Bronx Green-Up program bring community gardeners together to share experiences, techniques, and results. Training programs at the Garden's Home Gardening Center help aspiring community gardeners develop skills in topics that include garden design, composting, and pest management. Bronx Green-Up staff members also provide experience and advice to help local groups organize in order to gain increased community presence and have a public voice in decisions made about their neighborhoods.

With the assistance and support of the Bronx Green-Up program, more than a thousand Bronx community gardeners have claimed ownership of their neighborhoods, thereby enhancing the environment, strengthening communities, and enriching lives.

ADULT EDUCATION

The New York Botanical Garden operates the largest and most diverse continuing education program of any botanical garden in the country, if not the world. For more than eighty-five years, the Garden has helped people reach their educational goals. Today the program offers more than five hundred courses and serves more than 3,500 students.

Certificate programs are available in seven disciplines: botanical art and illustration, botany, floral design, gardening, landscape design, horticulture, and horticultural therapy. In addition, individual lectures and series as well as symposia on subjects such as garden design, garden history, botanical science, and plant ecology are offered on an ongoing basis at the Garden, in Manhattan, and at various suburban locations in the greater New York area.

The highly specialized School of Professional Horticulture is another of the Garden's educational offerings. Created in the 1950s by Thomas H. Everett, then head of horticulture, this program has trained hundreds of young adults for careers as fine gardeners, estate managers, nurserymen, and botanical garden professionals.

AFTERWORD: A LOOK TO THE FUTURE

It might be easy for a reader of this book, having been on an enchanted journey across 250 historic acres and seen some one million well-cared-for plants, to feel that the New York Botanical Garden is finished. Nothing could be further from the truth. As every gardener knows, the seasons come and go, and one's garden is always evolving, always changing for the better (or for the worse), and never finished.

And in many other areas of endeavor, our real work here in this mecca for plant lovers, plant students, and plant researchers has only begun. Fly in a light plane over the rain forests of Amazonia with a plant scientist, and you will learn from her that we know very little about the trees below—that in many cases scientists have not even given scientific names to the new species they are discovering every day. Ask a teacher in our children's garden here how best to teach a fifth-grade class about photosynthesis, and he will shrug his shoulders and say we still don't know. When visiting our Herbarium, quiz a curator about the northward movement of plants and animals in response to global warming, and she will say we think we possess the raw data that proves this theory, but we still have only primitive computer technology to analyze large amounts of information.

The world is changing (and parts of it are disappearing) very quickly. The botanical gardens of the world are charged with responsibility for collecting, growing, understanding, and teaching about the plants of the world. No one else is really doing so—no other institutions have the ability.

So we are working against time, trying to transform some of our Victorian-era methodology to "industrial strength." There aren't enough botanical gardens in the world. If you are so lucky as to have one in your community, treasure it—and help it out. If you live in a place where the plants are beautiful but no one pays attention, do something about it. Start a movement like Elizabeth Britton's—create a new haven for people and plants.

G.L./A.S.

Architectural elevation by Beyer Blinder Belle of the Enid A. Haupt Conservatory, which was restored in 1994–97

CONTRIBUTORS

Wilson Nolen, DCS, is chairman of the board of managers of the New York Botanical Garden. He has been involved with the Garden since the 1980s, serving as a member of its board since 1991, as chairman of the board since 2000, and as chairman of the *Campaign for a New Era: 2001–2007* since its inception. In May 2003, the Garden Club of America presented Nolen with its prestigious Medal of Honor for outstanding service to horticulture, citing his role in the renaissance of the Botanical Garden.

Gregory Long has spent thirty-five years in the management of New York City cultural institutions. After seven years with the New York Public Library, Long was made president and chief executive officer of the New York Botanical Garden in 1989. His administration has presided over a period of unprecedented growth and development at the Garden, during which more than half a billion dollars has been raised to restore and improve its buildings and landscapes, its programs, and its endowment.

Kim E. Tripp, Ph.D., is director of the New York Botanical Garden. She came to the Garden in 1999, when she was appointed vice president for horticulture and living collections, and in 2005 was promoted to director. In this role, she oversees all program areas—botanical science, horticulture, and education. Her academic interest is in conifer biology and conservation, and her publications include *The Year in Trees: Superb Woody Plants for Four-Season Gardens* (1995).

Todd Forrest is vice president for horticulture and living collections at the New York Botanical Garden. He came to the Garden in 1997 as an intern in botanical science and was promoted to vice president in 2005. His great love is woody plants, especially the Garden's tree and shrub collections.

Susan Fraser is director of the LuEsther T. Mertz Library. She has worked at the Library since 1984, becoming archivist and head of information services in 1993, and she was named director in 2003. In addition to her responsibilities in operating the Library, she oversees the exhibitions in the William D. Rondina and Giovanni Foroni LoFaro Gallery.

Barbara M. Thiers, Ph.D., has been director of the Garden's Herbarium since 2000. She is an expert bryologist (studying mosses and liverworts) who came to the Garden as an intern in botanical science in 1981, becoming manager of the cryptogamic collections in 1982. She has overseen the Garden's Virtual Herbarium project since it began in 1995.

Anne Skillion is senior editor in the publications office of the New York Public Library, where she has been on the staff since 1981. She is the developing and project editor for many illustrated books and exhibition catalogues, including the recent publications *Art Deco Bookbindings* (2004), *Before Victoria: Extraordinary Women of the British Romantic Era* (2005), and *Ehon: The Artist and the Book in Japan* (2006).

PRINCIPAL PHOTOGRAPHERS

Robert Benson, an architectural photographer, has been commissioned by many of the country's leading architects and has had his work published both nationally and internationally. He has two books to his credit, *The Connecticut River* and *I Will Sing Life.*

Mick Hales grew up in Devonshire, England. Hales's frequent travels to gardens around the world have produced images that are featured in twenty-two books and two hundred magazine articles. He recently completed a year-long study of the Garden that resulted in the exhibition "The Luminous Lens of Mick Hales: Photographs of The New York Botanical Garden."

Sara Cedar Miller has been the photographer for New York City's Central Park Conservancy since 1984 and its official historian since 1989. In 2003, she published *Central Park, An American Masterpiece: A Comprehensive History of the Nation's First Urban Park.* Her photographs have been published in books and periodicals around the world.

John Peden studied photography in San Francisco. The focus of his photographs has shifted from fashion to gardens and interiors. His work has been featured in the *New York Times Magazine, Gardens Illustrated,* and *Garden Design,* as well as in several publications of the New York Botanical Garden.

ACKNOWLEDGMENTS

New York Botanical Garden art director Marilan Lund has worked tirelessly for years to direct the photographers and assemble the visual material for this book. She deserves great thanks for ensuring its beauty and quality. We would also like to thank other staff members, including Margaret Falk, director of Plant Records and Information, for sharing her knowledge of the Garden's living collections; Brian Boom and Julie Taylor for their research and writing; Stephen Sinon, head of Information Services and Archives, for his research assistance; and Sally A. Leone for her editorial work.

We wish to thank Penelope Hobhouse, gardener, garden designer, and historian, for her assistance with the text. Also very helpful and generous were Edward O. Wilson, Ph.D., perhaps America's most celebrated biologist, teacher, and writer about biology; Neil Baldwin, distinguished and prolific American cultural historian and biographer; and Therese O'Malley, Ph.D., art historian, historian of botanical gardens, and associate dean at the Center for Advanced Study in the Visual Arts at the National Gallery of Art in Washington, D.C. We could not have undertaken this project without the collaboration and friendship of these four scholars.

We also wish to acknowledge the senior staff of the New York Botanical Garden for their untiring efforts on behalf of the institution: Kim E. Tripp, director of the Garden; J.V. Cossaboom, senior vice president and chief financial officer; and vice presidents Michael Adlerstein, Natalie Andersen, Michael Balick, Todd Forrest, Sally Gavin, Rosemary Ginty, Robert Heinisch, Lynn Holstein, Barbara Ifshin, Tim Landi, Karl Lauby, Susan Maier, and Dennis Stevenson.

At Abrams/New York, we are grateful to editor Barbara Burn and designer Robert McKee for their fine professional work in creating this elegant book.

G.L./A.S.

Greenhouse in *Grotesque Architecture* by William Wrighte, 1767, from the Elizabeth Kals Reilley Collection of the LuEsther T. Mertz Library

BIBLIOGRAPHY

GENERAL

Bartholomew, James. *The Magic of Kew*. New York: New Amsterdam, 1988.

Bry, Charleene, Marshall R. Crosby, and Peter Loewer. *A World of Plants: The Missouri Botanical Garden*. New York: Abrams, 1989.

Chicago Horticultural Society. *A Garden for All Seasons: Chicago Botanic Garden*. Chicago: Chicago Horticultural Society, 1990.

Desmond, Ray. *Kew: The History of the Royal Botanic Gardens*. London: Harvill Press with the Royal Botanic Gardens, Kew, 1995.

De Koning, Jan. "The Development of Botany in the Sixteenth Century" in Alessandro Minelli, ed. *The Botanical Garden of Padua 1545–1995*. Venice: Marsilio Editore, S.P.A., 1995.

Filler, Martin. "Evergreen Treasure" *House & Garden* (June 2002): 84.

Gilbert, Lionel. *The Royal Botanic Gardens, Sydney: A History 1816–1985*. Melbourne and New York: Oxford University Press, 1986.

Gothein, Marie Luise Schroeter. *A History of Garden Art*. London: Dent, [1928].

Grove, Carol. *Henry Shaw's Victorian Landscapes: The Missouri Botanical Garden and Tower Grove Park*. Amherst: University of Massachusetts Press, in association with Library of American History, 2005.

Henty, Carol. *For the People's Pleasure: Australia's Botanic Gardens*. New York: Rizzoli International Publications, 1989.

Hepper, F. Nigel. *Kew, Gardens for Science & Pleasure*. Owings Mills, Md.: Stemmer House Publishers, 1982.

Hyams, Edward, and William MacQuitty. *Great Botanic Gardens of the World*. New York: Macmillan, 1969.

Kimmelman, Michael. "Where the Art Grows on Trees (and Everywhere Else)." *The New York Times*, December 30, 2005, E35–E36.

Klinkenborg, Verlyn. "Visit the New York Botanical Garden now, and learn about the potent appeal of bare nature." *Town & Country* (December 2005): 235–42.

Lawrence, George H. M. *The Historical Role of the Botanic Garden*. Longwood Program Seminars. Newark, Del.: The University of Delaware, 1968–69.

Loxton, Howard, ed. *The Garden: A Celebration*. New York: Barron's, 1991.

Nelson, E. Charles, and Eileen M. McCracken. *The Brightest Jewel: A History of the National Botanic Gardens, Glasnevin, Dublin*. Kilkenny: Boethius Press, 1987.

Prest, John. *The Garden of Eden: The Botanic Garden and the Re-Creation of Paradise*. New Haven and London: Yale University Press, 1981.

Soderstrom, Mary. *Recreating Eden: A Natural History of Botanical Gardens*. Montreal: Vehicule Press, 2001.

Tanner, Odgen, and Adele Auchincloss. *The New York Botanical Garden: An Illustrated Chronicle of Plants and People*. New York: Walker and Co., 1991.

Veendorp, H., and L. G. M. Baas Becking. *The Development of the Gardens of Leyden University*. Haarlem: Ex Typographiia Enschedaiana, 1938.

Visentini, Margherita Azzi. *L'Orto Botanico di Padova e il giardino del Rinascimento*. Milan: Polifilo, 1984.

Wyman, Donald. "The Arboretum and Botanical Gardens of North America." *Chronica Botanica* 10 (1947): 442–44.

A SPLENDID NATURAL SITE

An act to provide for the establishment of a Botanic Garden and Museum and Arboretum in Bronx Park, in the City of New York, and to incorporate the New York Botanical Garden for carrying on the same." Eight-page brochure. 1891.

Dunkak, Harry. "The Lorillard Family of Westchester County: Tobacco, Property and Nature." *Westchester Historian* 71, no. 3. Elmsford, N.Y.: Westchester County Historical Society, 1995.

Glenn, William H. *Guide to Geology: The New York Botanical Garden*. Bronx: New York Botanical Garden, 1978.

A Guide to the New York Botanical Garden. Bronx: New York Botanical Garden, 1964.

Mickulas, Peter Philip. "Giving, Getting and Growing: Philanthropy, Science, and the New York Botanical Garden, 1888–1929." Ph.D. dissertation, Rutgers University, 2003.

Mullaly, John. *The New Parks Beyond the Harlem: Nearly 4,000 Acres of Free Playground for the People*. New York: Record & Guide, 1887.

A FLOWERY TAPESTRY: GARDENS AND BORDERS

Corning, Elizabeth P. *Guide to the Native Plant Garden*. Bronx: New York Botanical Garden, 1982, 1967.

Everett, Thomas H. [and members of the American Rock Garden Society]. *Rock and Alpine Gardens*. Millwood, N.Y.: Hudson Valley Chapter of the American Rock Garden Society, 1992.

Halpin, Anne Moyer, and Robert Bartolomei. *Master Gardener: Rock Gardens*. New York: Clarkson Potter, 1999.

Hubbard, Juliet Alsop. *A Walk in the Wild: Native Plants and Their Habitats at the New York Botanical Garden*. Bronx: New York Botanical Garden, 1991.

Mickel, John, and Joseph M. Beitel. *Hardy Ferns: A Guide to the F. Gordon Foster Hardy Fern Collection at the New York Botanical Garden*. Bronx: New York Botanical Garden, 1987.

Ruggiero, Michael, and Ruth Rogers Clausen. *Perennial Gardening*. New York: Pantheon Books, 1994.

Utterback, Christine, and Michael Ruggiero. *Master Gardener: Reliable Roses*. New York: Clarkson Potter, 1999.

NEW YORK'S CRYSTAL PALACE: THE ENID A. HAUPT CONSERVATORY

Appel, Allan. *A Walk through A World of Plants: The Enid A. Haupt Conservatory at the New York Botanical Garden*. Bronx: New York Botanical Garden, 1997.

Falk, Margaret, and Anne Steinbrook, eds. *All Aboard! A Tour of the Holiday Train Show at the New York Botanical Garden*. Bronx: New York Botanical Garden, 2003.

Jones Jr., Malcolm. "Eden Without End." *Preservation* (March/April 1997): 97.

Koebner, Linda. "Green House." *Landscape Architecture* 87, no. 5 (May 1997): 60.

The Orchid Show at the New York Botanical Garden. Photographs by John Peden. Bronx: Shop in the Garden Books, New York Botanical Garden, 2004.

DEFINING A LANDSCAPE: TREE AND SHRUB COLLECTIONS

Forrest, Todd. *The Arthur and Janet Ross Conifer Arboretum*. Bronx: New York Botanical Garden, 2004.

Forrest, Todd. *The Benenson Ornamental Conifers*. Bronx: New York Botanical Garden, 2004.

New York Botanical Garden Forest Management Plan. Bronx: New York Botanical Garden, 2001.

Raver, Anne. "Forever Green: in the Bronx, a jungle is tamed, and a collection of conifers emerges." *The New York Times*, October 28, 2004, F6.

Tripp, Kim E., and Allen Coombes. *The Complete Book of Shrubs: A Step-by-Step Guide to Planting, Cultivating, and Designing with Shrubs*. New York: Reader's Digest, 1998.

Tripp, Kim E., and J.C. Raulston. *The Year in Trees: Superb Woody Plants for Four-Season Gardens*. Portland, Ore.: Timber Press, 1995.

NOTABLE ARCHITECTURE

Building a Borough: Architecture and Planning in the Bronx, 1890–1940. Bronx: Bronx Museum of the Arts, 1986.

Collins, Glenn. "A Marriage of Old and New, With Flowers, A 21st-Century Greenhouse Joins a Domed Bronx Classic." *The New York Times*, September 24, 2004, B1–B3.

"Descriptive Guide to the Grounds, Buildings and Collections." *Bulletin of the New York Botanical Garden* 5 (December 1906). Published for the Garden by the New Era Printing Company.

Gill, Brendan. "The New York Botanical Garden at 100." *Architectural Digest*. November 1991.

Hix, John. *The Glasshouse*. London: Phaidon, 1996.

Woods, May, and Arete Swartz Warren. *Glass Houses: A History of Greenhouses, Orangeries and Conservatories*. New York: Rizzoli, 1988.

SEVEN MILLION SPECIMENS AND COUNTING: THE WILLIAM AND LYNDA STEERE HERBARIUM

Altschul, Siri von Reis. "Exploring the Herbarium." *Scientific American* 236, no. 5 (1977): 96–104.

Brittonia. Bronx: New York Botanical Garden, 1931–.

Fleming, Mary, and Rupert Barneby. "Treasures of the Garden's Herbarium, III: The Bryophytes of William Mitten." *The Garden Journal* 14, no. 3 (1964): 146–48.

Griffiths, Mark. "Growth of New York's museum of plants." *The Times* (London), April 9, 2002, 40.

Holmgren, Patricia, Jacquelyn Kallunki, and Barbara Thiers. "A short description of the collections of the New York Botanical Garden Herbarium (NY)." *Brittonia* 48, no. 3 (1996): 285–96.

Holmgren, Patricia K., Noel H. Holmgren, and Lisa C. Barnett, eds. *Index Herbariorum. The Herbaria of the World*. Bronx: Published and distributed for the International Association for Plant Taxonomy by the New York Botanical Garden, 1990.

In Celebration of Plant Science, May 1–July 31, 2002, Grand Opening of the LuEsther T. Mertz Library and the William and Lynda Steere Herbarium, May 1, 2002. Bronx: New York Botanical Garden, 2002.

Journal of the New York Botanical Garden. Bronx: New York Botanical Garden, 1900–1950.

Raver, Anne. "Twigs and Texts With Stories to Tell." *The New York Times*, April 25, 2002, F4.

A TREASURY OF BOTANICAL KNOWLEDGE: THE LuESTHER T. MERTZ LIBRARY

Anderson, Frank J. *An Illustrated History of the Herbals*. New York: Columbia University Press, 1977.

Anderson, Frank J. *A Treasury of Flowers: Rare Illustrations from the Collection of the New York Botanical Garden*. Boston: Little, Brown, 1990.

Blunt, Wilfrid. *The Art of Botanical Illustration*. London: Collins, 1950.

Eustis, Elizabeth S. *European Pleasure Gardens: Rare Books and Prints of Historic Landscape Design from the Elizabeth K. Reilley Collection*. Bronx: New York Botanical Garden, 2003.

Eustis, Elizabeth S., John F. Reed, and David L. Andrews. *Plants and Gardens Portrayed: Rare and Illustrated Books from the LuEsther T. Mertz Library: An Exhibition in the William D. Rondina and Giovanni Foroni LoFaro Gallery*. Bronx: New York Botanical Garden, 2002.

Fraser, Susan, and John F. Reed. *A Reader's Guide to the LuEsther T. Mertz Library*. Bronx: New York Botanical Garden, 2002.

O'Malley, Therese. *Glasshouses: The Architecture of Light and Air: An Exhibition in the William D. Rondina and Giovanni Foroni LoFaro Gallery*. Bronx: New York Botanical Garden, 2005.

Raphael, Sandra. *An Oak Spring Sylva: A Selection of the Rare Books on Trees in the Oak Spring Garden Library*. Upperville, Va.: Oak Spring Garden Library (distributed by Yale University Press), 1989.

Rix, Martyn. *The Art of the Plant World: The Great Botanical Illustrators and Their Work*. Woodstock, N.Y.: Overlook Press, 1981.

Sitwell, Sacheverell. *Great Flower Books, 1700–1900: A Bibliographical Record of Two Centuries of Finely Illustrated Flower Books*. London, Collins, 1956; New York: Atlantic Monthly Press, 1990.

Tongiorgi Tomasi, Lucia. *An Oak Spring Flora: Flower Illustration from the Fifteenth Century to the Present Time: A Selection of the Rare Books, Manuscripts and Works of Art in the Collection of Rachel Lambert Mellon*. Upperville, Va.: Oak Spring Garden Library (distributed by Yale University Press), 1997.

FROM THE BRONX TO BORNEO: THE INTERNATIONAL PLANT SCIENCE CENTER

Before the Green Is Gone: A New Century of Biodiversity Research at the New York Botanical Garden. Bronx: New York Botanical Garden, 2005.

Boom, Brian. "One Hundred Years of Botanical Research and Scholarly Publishing at the New York Botanical Garden." *Brittonia* 48, no. 3 (1996): 281–84.

Garden News. Bronx: New York Botanical Garden, 1991–.

The International Plant Science Center at the New York Botanical Garden, 2001–2007. Bronx: New York Botanical Garden, 2000.

Additional publications can be found on the Garden's Web site at http://sciweb.nybg.org/science2/

A TEACHING GARDEN

Bronx Green-Up: An Outreach Program of the New York Botanical Garden. Bronx: New York Botanical Garden, 1995.

Daly, Douglas C., and Elizabeth A. Christy. *Neighborhood Composting in New York City*. New York: Council on the Environment of New York City, c. 1978.

Green-Up Times: The Newsletter of the New York Botanical Garden's Bronx Green-Up Program, 1989–99.

Hassell, Malve von. *The Struggle for Eden: Community Gardens in New York City*. Westport, Conn.: Bergin & Garvey, 2002.

Magnolia
Collection

Howell Family Garden

BRONX RIVER

Native Forest

WATERFALL

FOREST TRAIL

Hester Bridge

Twin Lakes

Native Forest

FOREST TRAIL

Pfizer Laboratory

Rock Garden

Education
Building

Liasson Narcissus
Collection

Native Plant
Garden

Steere
Herbarium

Mertz
Library

ROCK GARDEN PATH

Mitsubishi Wild
Wetland Trail

Ross
Lecture
Hall

KAZIMIROFF BOULEVARD

GARDEN WAY

Tulip Tree Allée

Reflecting Pool

Shop in the
Garden

Everett Children's
Adventure Garden

WATSON DRIVE

PERENNIAL GARDEN WAY

Leon Levy
Visitor Center

Mosholu Gate

Cafe

Ross Conifer
Arboretum

Conservatory Gate
Main Entrance

DAYLILY/DAFFODIL WALK

Luce Herb
Garden

Garden
Cafe

Irwin Perennial
Garden

Ladies' Border

Metro-North Railroad
Botanical Garden Station

Haupt Conservatory

Home Gardening
Center

CONSERVATORY DRIVE

KAZIMIROFF BOULEVARD

Lilac
Collection

Rockefeller
Rose
Garden

Nolen Greenhouses
Bourke-Sullivan Display House

BRONX RIVER PARKWAY

Cherry
Collection

Maple
Collection

Benenson Ornamental Conifers

Snuff
Mill

FOREST TRAIL

SNUFF MILL ROAD

BRONX RIVER

AZALEA WAY

Crabapple
Collection

Clay Family
Picnic Pavilions

Daffodil Hill

FORDHAM ROAD

David Cain

Leon Levy Visitor Center

Enid A. Haupt Conservatory

LuEsther T. Mertz Library

INDEX

Page numbers in *italics* refer to illustrations.

Page 10: *Prospectus Horti Academici Lugduno Batavi* from Herman Boerhaave (1668–1738), *Index Alter Plantarum...* (Leiden: J. van der Aa, 1727); **page 12:** *Orto Botanico di Padova* from Roberto de Visiani (1800–1878), *L'Orto Botanico di Padova…* (Padua: A. Sicca, 1842); **page 13:** *Prospectus Horti Medici Pisani* from Michel Angelo Tilli (1655–1740), *Catalogus plantarum Horti Pisani* (Florence: Tartinium & Franchium, 1723), and *Hortus Botanicus The Phisick Garden at Oxon* from *Oxonia Illustrata* (Oxford: L. Lichfield, 1675) (print from collection of Gregory Long); **page 14:** *Vitis vinifera* from Elizabeth Blackwell (fl. 1737), *Curious Herbal* (London: J. Nourse, 1739–51); **page 19:** Boundary map of the New York Botanical Garden, 1895, by Calvert Vaux (1824–1895) and Samuel Parsons (1844–1923) (Archives of the New York Botanical Garden); **page 38:** *Aquilegia* from *The Floral Magazine* (London: L. Reeve & Co., 1873); **page 39:** *Monarda* from Christoph Jacob Trew (1695–1769), *Plantae Selectae* (Nuremberg, 1750–73), and *Campanula* from Pierre-Joseph Redouté (1759–1840), *Choix des plus belles fleurs* (Paris: C.L.F. Panckoucke, 1827); **page 50:** *Stout Daylilies,* watercolor by Eleanor Clarke, c. 1930 (Archives of the New York Botanical Garden); **page 59:** *Gentiana acaulis* from William Curtis (1746–1799), *Curtis's botanical magazine* (London: S. Couchman, 1793–1801); **page 71:** *Veratrum scapo fistulos* [Helonius bullato] from Trew, *Plantae Selectae;* **page 71:** *Cimifuga racemosa* from Joseph Carson (1808–1876), *Illustrations of medical botany…* (Philadelphia: R. P. Smith, 1847), and *Uvularia perfoliata* from Pierre-Joseph Redouté, *Les Liliacées* (Paris: Didot jeune, 1802–16); **page 72:** Beatrix Farrand (1872–1959), Rose Garden plan, January 5, 1916 (Archives of the New York Botanical Garden); **page 80:** *Rosa eglanteria* from Pierre Joseph Redouté, *Les Roses* (Paris: F. Didot, 1817–24); **page 85:** *Paeonia mouton* from Aimé Bonpland (1773–1858), *Description des plantes rares…* (Paris: P. Didot l'aine, 1813); **page 94:** *Mauritia armata* from Karl Friedrich Philipp von Martius (1794–1868), *Historia naturalis palmarum* (Leipzig: T. O. Weigel, 1823–50); **page 98:** *Bromelia* from Trew, *Plantae Selectae;* **page 103:** *Papaya* from Trew, *Plantae Selectae;* **page 106:** *Vaccinium salignum, V. serpens* from Sir Joseph Dalton Hooker (1817–1911), *Illustrations of Himalayan plants* (London: L. Reeve, 1855); **page 110:** *Opuntia species,* watercolor by Mary E. Eaton, c. 1920 (Archives of the New York Botanical Garden); **page 113:** *Kiku chrysthanthemum* [Ori-taki-shiba] from Kanezumi Imai, *Kikka Meiji-sen* (Tokyo, 1891); **page 125:** *Cattleya dowiana* from Robert Warner (1815–1896), *Select orchidaceous plants* (London: L. Reeve, 1862–65), and *Cattleya guttata var. russelliana* from Sir Joseph Dalton Hooker (1817–1911), *Century of orchidaceous plants* (London: Reeve and Benham, 1851); **page 132:** *Victoria regia* from Sir Joseph Dalton Hooker, *Victoria regia* (London: Reeve and Benham, 1851); **page 137:** *Pinus strobus* from François Andre Michaux (1770–1855), *Histoire des arbres forestiers* (Paris: C. Haussmann et d'Hautel, 1810–13); **page 143:** *Sequoia Wellingtonia* (The Two Guardsmen) from Edward Ravenscroft (1816–1890), *The Pinetum Britannicum* (Edinburgh: W. Blackwood, 1884); **page 145:** *Liriodendrum* from Trew, *Plantae Selectae;* **page 146:** *Rhododendron schlippenbachii,* from *Curtis's botanical magazine* (London: Reeve Brothers, 1894); **page 158:** *Cedar of Lebanon* from

Allgemeines teutsches Garten-magazin (Weimar 1794–1804), and *Taxus baccata* from Johann Simon Kerner (1759–1840), *Figures des plantes economiques* (Stuttgart: Christofle Frederic Cotta, 1786–96); **page 162:** *Lilas* from Redouté, *Choix des plus belles fleurs;* **page 170:** *Magnolia altissima* from Mark Catesby (1683–1749), *Hortus Europae Americanus* (London: J. Millan, 1767); **page 176:** *White oak and Red oak* from François André Michaux, *The North American Sylva* (Philadelphia: Thomas Dobson and Solomon Conrad, 1817–19); **page 190:** Library building façade elevation by Robert Gibson, 1897 (Archives of the New York Botanical Garden); **page 214:** *Amaryllis Josephinae* from Redouté, *Les Liliacées;* **page 215:** *Dioscorides* title page from *De Materia Medica* (1518), Matthaeus Platearius (d. 1161); **page 216:** Konrad von Megenberg (1309–1374), *Hye nach volget das půch der nature...* (Augsburg: Hans Bumler, 1475); **page 217:** *Circa instans,* manuscript (Salerno, c. 1190); **page 218:** *Kuchenschell* [Pasque flower] from Otto Brunfels (1488–1534), *Contrafayt Kreuterbuch…* (Strasbourg: J. Schott, 1532–1537); **page 219:** *Morenia Pöppigiana* from Martius, *Historia naturalis palmarum;* **page 220:** *Laminaria bongardiana palmata* from Aleksandr Postels (1801–1871), *Illustrationes algarum…*(Saint Petersburg: E. Pranz, 1840); **page 221:** *Cereus gracilis scandens* and *Cedrus foliis nigidis* from Trew, *Plantae Selectae;* **page 222:** *Prospect des Bosquet mit einer Parterre von Waase* from Salomon Kleiner (1703–1759), *Viereley Vorstellungen…* (Augsburg; Johann Andreas Pfeffel, c. 1730); **page 223:** *Colossal Statue of the Apennines* from Stefano della Bella (1610–1664), [Six views of the Villa Medici at Pratolino] (Florence, c. 1651/53), Frontispiece from Giovanni Battista Falda (1640–1678), *Li Giardini di Roma…* (Rome: G. G. de Rossi, 1683); **page 224:** Whitton, *Seat of Samuel Prime Esq.* from Humphry Repton (1752–1818), "Red Book" (1796); **page 225:** Binding from Sophie Bledsloe Herrick, *The Wonders of Plant Life Under the Microscope* (New York: G. P. Putnam's Sons, 1883), and Mico Chlucco, *The Long Warior or King of the Siminoles* from William Bartram (1739–1823), *Travels through North & South Carolina…* (Philadelphia: James & Johnson, 1791); **page 226:** Title page engraving from Nikolaus Joseph von Jacquin (1727–1817), *Selectarum Stirpium Americanarum Historia* (Vienna: Ex Officinia Krausiana, 1763); **page 227:** *Black oak* from Michaux, *The North American Sylva,* title page from John M. Ives, *The New England Book of Fruits* (Salem: W. and S. B. Ives, 1847), *Early Joe Apple,* watercolor painted for James H. Watts, Rochester, N.Y. by Joseph Prestele, c. 1850, and *Flowers from Seeds* from C. H. Lippincott nursery catalogue cover (Minneapolis, 1883); **page 229:** [Mushrooms], watercolor by Mary E. Eaton, c. 1930 (Archives of the New York Botanical Garden), and *Mollua populifolia* from Karl Friedrich Philipp von Martius (1794–1868), *Flora Brasiliensis* (Munich and Leipzig: R. Oldenbourg, 1840–1906).